OPTIONS TRADING

The Ultimate, Simple & Practical Options Trading Guide to Start Investing Consciously

Anthony Wilson

TABLE OF CONTENTS:

Introduction

This book is for any person who is interested in trading. It is meant for any trader whether they are new or have experience in trading.

This book is meant to give access to all the information needed to survive and be successful in options trading. If you had a hard time knowing what options trading is, worry not. You will know what options trading means, the best platform for it, and the different terms used.

More information is shared on the basic concepts applied in options trading, such as why it is important to use options, and there are practical examples to illustrate all that. For beginners, there is enough information on how to start options trading, the capital needed the strategies to apply, and how the whole process works. You will also have access to all the effective tools. Money management is very important, and that topic is clearly explained too as well as the mistakes to avoid in options trading.

Chapter 1:
What Is Option Trading?

An option is an agreement that enables you to purchase and sell specific stock trading amounts at a particular price within a particular trading time before the date of expiration avails. Options exist in two kinds: call options and put options. We are going to dive into the deep content of the mentioned kinds later on in the book.

The Best Options Trading Platform

There exist different trading platforms for options trading. Picking out a particular trading platform is not so easy. The selected trading site should first correspond to what you want to major on and its efficiency. Let us explore some of the best platforms for options trading with different features, and I hope that you spot the one that fascinates you:

TD Ameritrade: It has been ranked the best trading platform recently due to its reasonable pricing, excellent beginner sources, and top-notch platform suitable for professional options traders and experts. This kind of platform has something good for everyone, as depicted by its best options. Trading with TD Ameritrade is so worth it as depicted by its great platform, good learning materials, in-depth research, and better customer support.

Below are some of the reasons why most traders venture into this kind of platform:

Creative platforms - It is much detailed and this eventually makes the trader much informed, which is a great opportunity to the beginners and the experienced options traders.

- Extensive product access
- Adequate guidance
- 24/7 support
- No hidden fees
- Easy to use because it is pretty much simplified and therefore used by a good number of beginners

Trade Station: Experts are highly recommended to engage in this particular kind of platform as it costs $5 in each trade and $0.50 in each contract.

Charles Schwab Platform: This kind of platform mainly targets the novice in options trading. It provides a great experience and awesome customer service as evidenced by the in-depth research with great educational materials.
Unique order types are believed to be highly involved.

Ally Invest: When the need to minimize options trading costs is so high, the Ally Invest trading platform becomes a favorable option. A low kind of investment can be considered when commencing trading without worrying about the issues of big minimum balances. This platform is commonly known for cheap trades, rock bottom rates, availability of easy entry points, and stellar ratings. Moreover, Ally Invests has no minimum amount required in their accounts.

Robinhood: This is a great platform for beginners to start from because limited risks are involved. Since there is no trading fee, options can be purchased and sold with the exception of interfering with the initial investment. Robinhood does not provide much of learning sources and research tools information, but if you are sure to get some

good books, this trading platform is going to be much friendly.
Robinhood is loved as a good options trading platform because it is pretty much user-friendly and there are no commission fees involved.

Interactive Brokers: This platform is suitable for active traders who arelikely to get involved in frequent small trades and not really for passive traders with just a few trades per year. This site is rated the best in providing the best commission rates.

Lightspeed Trader: This platform focuses on the active and experienced traders as it offers professional-grade trading platforms. There is low pricing for large-volume traders, and the right site for various brokerage needs to be involved during options.

*E*Trade*: It supports both novice and experts

involved in options trading. This platform is well-detailed and contains quite a large amount of data and research tools that aid in building advanced options trading chains and trading ladders. It is common to the active kind of traders because of various reasons such as no commission fees, and the site is pretty much detailed, hence making the traders quite informed and their low minimum account balance value.

Gatsby: This platform is known to be best for retail investors, traders that are new to options, social traders, and millennial traders involved in options trading. It is adequately detailed with options trading information enough to give a particular novice trader the courage and skills to commence options trading without being such a mess.

Fidelity: In this platform, traders are guided in the right direction, and resources needed along the way are also provided. Large chunks of research tools and learning resources are available for education and guidance to ease the options trading process for the option of novice traders. Moreover, the fidelity platform offers phone support throughout in case of any complications experienced by any options trader. Fidelity platform is famous for great research and the necessary tools needed in options trading. It has a high functioning site and very good at research. However, not all tools present to this site are available to all the users.

Vanguard: This platform is best for investors who are planning to retire with the intention of long-term options trading and high volume earnings.

AvaTrade: This is an online site offering its customers with various contracts that they would initiate options trading between various buyers and sellers.

This site is legit and reliable and it has been fully approved by the government and even termed as a good trading policy. It targets all kinds of traders such as the novice, experienced, intermediate, and many more.

Options Trading Vs. Stock Trading

There is a big difference between options trading and stock trading.

Stock represents partial ownership of the company implying that when you purchase a stock, you are normally a part of the company. On the other hand, options trading is merely any ownership of a certain company; it is a contract involving a trader and another party that allows the trader to purchase or sell a certain amount of stock at a particular price within a specific period. The market may be so volatile but the strike prices reads are so high, and when the market activities are depicted to be calm, the strike prices may eventually be so down.

Let us look at some of the major differences between options trading and stock trading:

1. Options tend to expire as depicted by the availability of expiration dates, while, on the other hand, stocks are much durable since they are properties of the company and bear no expiration dates. Therefore, stock trading is likely to happen for a longer period as compared to stock trading.

2. Options derive the actual value from the value of the other assets involved during options trading, whereas stocks have a definite actual value that is fully recognized by the company in question.

3. In the options trading activities, traders just have the full rights of the value amount. On the other hand, stock trading gives the traders gain full ownership of the property involved during trading activities.

4. In options trading, the market predictability does not necessarily depend on the rates of supply and demand levels as compared to stock trading. With this in mind, the options trader is unlikely to predict what is happens to the market but he/she can, however, check on the volatility of the market.

5. Options are much cheaper than stock. Money is so fundamental in trading and is always the biggest motivation in any kind of trading activity. Options are less expensive since the trader gets to acquire 100 shares of the equity during trading. Moreover, the cost of grasping an option contract is much cheaper as compared to purchasing and the underlying stock, and the trader acquires more amounts of benefits as compared to stock trading.

6. Options are normally a great leverage tool in maximizing the amounts of profits gained

during a particular trading period as compared to stock trading. This is evident in the collection of various amounts of premiums during the issuance of contracts hence increasing the amounts of profits collected in options trading as compared to stock trading.

7. Options trading is much good at flexibility as compared to stock trading as evident in its tactical operations that happen frequently in various trading activities. Traders can make smaller investments that lead to good amounts of profits and fewer risks involved during a particular period. On the other hand, stock trading calls for good investments with multiple amounts of risks over an unspecified period.

8. Another point is that options have a great chance of limiting the risks that are likely to be involved during trading, as compared to

stock trading, where risk is pretty much unlimited during the unspecified period of trading.

9. Options trading can better for you if your timing is okay, and as an options trader, you will be able to acquire larger amounts of profits during the contract as compared to when you would be involved in options trading.

10. Options trading allows a particular option trader to bet where the market will not go–an activity that is not allowed in stock trading. The advantage of this opportunity is that there are higher chances of success than betting on where the market will go.

Terminologies Used in Options Trading

Option - It is a contract that allows an investor to purchase and sell a specific trading stock at a particular price within a particular period.

Call option - This is an equity agreement that awards a buyer the chance to purchase 100 particular shares at a particular strike price within a specified time. A seller is also needed to sell off the stock at a particular price if the option gets exercised.

Equity option - It is a kind of option that gives the owner, who happens to be the buyer, the chance to purchase and sell any available stock in the trading market at a specific share during a particular period before the expiration date is reached.

Commission - This is the fee charged in an options trading market after option orders have been executed on a securities exchange.

Strike price - This is the actual amount of price in which you choose to sell or buy options when you decide to exercise an option in the market.

Expiry date - This is the actual date–day, month, or year–to which a particular options trading contract becomes invalid and null.

Premium - It describes the price of an option, particularly the entire dollar value of the contract during a certain trading period.

Time decay - This is the erosion period when the value of time of a specific option diminishes as the expiration date reaches.

Put option - The kind of option where a buyer is given the privilege to sell 100 shares at a constant price before the expiration date. On another hand, the seller of a put option is required to purchase stock at a particular price if the trading option gets exercised at all.

Volume -This is the number of contracts that have been traded during a particular options trading period.

Holder - The specific owner of the contract is referred to as the holder in options trading.

Long Option - This simply implies having purchased an option at online transactions and therefore own it.

Short Option - This means to have sold the option in an opening transaction.

Change - The percentage term price of the last hour's sale in the options market.

Front-month - When the expiration of two months is involved in options trading, the month nearer in time is normally considered.

Index option - This is an option contract where the index is the underlying stock and not shares of any specific stock.

Time value - It describes the value to which time is attributable in options before a particular expiration date is reached.

Volatility - This is the actual fluctuation of prices of stocks in options trading where the stock prices keep rising and falling within time hence making it hard for traders to predict on future likely activities.

Contract - This is an agreement set between a buyer trader and a seller trader during a particular options trading activity.

Underlying asset - This is the 100 shares of stock that are involved in a particular agreement during a specified time.

Ask price - This is the lowest price that is being advertised in the options trading that anyone is willing to accept when selling a particular option at a particular period.

Last sale - It is the latest price that a certain option trader has traded within options trading.

Open interest - This is the number of the option that has been sold and also the ones that have not been brought back or in any case, exercise.

Bullish - This term is particularly referring to an investor who believes that a specific stock price will go higher or simply the market will rise higher.

Bearish - This term, on the other hand, describes a trader who believes that the market prices will do lower or the market will experience a downfall at a particular trading activity in a specific period.

Break-even point - This is the specific price that an underlying asset must reach to avoid the option buyer from acquiring losses if at all they decided to exercise the option.

Premium - This is the amount of income received by an option trader as he or she writes a contract off to another party.

Downside risk - This is the estimation of a particular downfall marketprice that is likely to be experienced by the market during the end of a particular trading period.

Implied volatility - This is an estimation of the future likelihood market volatility by analyzing the market status through the current activities occurring at the options trading market. Some traders get to use this as one of their strategies the options trading market to acquire large chunks of profits.

Index option - This is a kind of an option contract whose underlyingsecurity is an index and not shares of any specific stock.

Writing an option - This is to sell a call or put option contract that has been not possessed by any other trader in the market.

M*ean* - This is a mathematical operation where the total sum of observations in the market is divided by the particular number of observations in the market. The mean is used to provide data on various market values and the market standard deviation.

Spread - This is an option position established when a purchase of one option is established and a sale of an option too using the same underlying asset available in the trading market.

Historical volatility -This is analyzing the actual volatility of the past market occurrences and making the necessary helpful strategies and learning in your trading plan.

Credit - It is any value amount received in a particular trading account from the financial benefits experienced in various options trading activities. The profits and multiple benefits feed the trading accounts.

Debit - This is any amount of cash paid out to purchase an option during a particular trading period.

Horizontal - This is a term describing the options of the same strike price experienced in different months.

At the money - This term is used to describe the nearest price to the equity price during a particular trading moment.

Vertical - It is a term describing the options of different strike prices experienced in a particular month.

Resistance - This is a particular level where the equity price can not beyond any way higher, meaning that that particular price is the actual price limit.

Big chicken trade - This is a term used to describe a series of bull call calendars and the bear put calendars.

Ex-dividend - This is the actual date in which the stock enters the options trading market with the absence of dividends.

Selling to open - This ideally describes the selling of a particular option to open a position.

Selling to close - Selling a close means selling a specific option with the desire to close a particular position during options trading.

In the money - All the strike prices possess some intrinsic value where for a call, all strike prices are below the equity price whereas, for a put, all prices are the ones above the price of the equity.

Bid spread- This is the actual difference between the asking price and the bid price for a given option during a particular options trading period.

Dip in the money - This is a term used to refer to multiple in-the-money occurrences that have been experienced in a particular trading period in the options market.

Option spread - It is established by buying and selling equal amounts of options of a similar class with the same underlying security. However, the strike prices and expiration dates of the options are different.

Stock - It is described as a portion of a particular company belonging or ownership.

Margin - This is a particular amount of loan offered by a particular broker of a specific trader during a particular trading period.

Trading platform - This is a general trading site that traders interact with while making trading moves, buying, selling, and any other trading activities. Trading platforms consist of various kinds according to different variety of interests, and a trader gets to pick on a site in which he or she is most comfortable with.

Chapter 2:
The Basic Concepts of Options

For you to succeed, you need the basic knowledge of what you want to do for it will help you on how to do things the right way with less trouble. To fit in the options trading game, you need to know the basic knowledge about this type of trading to be on the safer side. In this chapter, we shall take a look at the strategies you can use, the types of options, how it works, and its drawbacks.

Strategies Used in Options Trading

Strategies are the set of guidelines you need to follow to achieve amazing results in what you are doing, and options trading has its strategies, too. Let us now dig deeper into a number of the strategies that you need to implement.

Covered call strategy. It is a market transaction where an individual, mostly an investor who is offering call options for sale, owns the same size as the market trade. It is executed when the individual with the long term asset writes the call options on the asset. Covered call strategy is a popular strategy because of its capability to minimize risks and promote income generation.

It is mostly applied when you, as an investor, have an asset with a short term and short position, wanting to hold it for long for you to receive the options premiums. A seller who has amazing knowledge on covered call strategygets higher profits as compared to other strategies. The drawback of this strategy is that an individual does not receive full options premium when the stock rises above the strike price.

Long straddle strategy. This is an options strategy where a trader purchases an asset that has both the long standard options and put-call. Also, the agreed price plus the time of expiry are normally similar. This strategy generates massive profits by having long put and call options. The long call practice in the market happens when long put expires, and there is a rise in the price of the instrument. Moreover, the long put is practiced only in the fall of the stock's price scenario. You are advised to use this strategy when you think the volatility of the stock will be significant through the trade term. You suffer losses if your underlying stock comes in between the upper and lower breakeven point.

Short straddle strategy. It is a risky strategy that is the vice versa of the long straddle options strategy. As an investor, you are advised to apply this strategy when there are chances of low volatility in the market. You are likely to suffer from significant losses when the stock behaves significantly in the market. The investor generates income and holds on the premium when the stock behavior in the market does not have much change in either direction.

Long strangle strategy. How does long strangle strategy work? Here is the answer to it. An investor normally purchases out of money standard options and puts calls simultaneously on the instrument with a similar time of expiry. Out of the money call option is a call option with a lower market price than the price agreed on an asset. Conversely, out of the money put option is a market situation in the case that an asset has a price above the strike price.

Most of the investors who apply this strategy have the belief that the asset will have a huge change in its behavior but are not sure in which direction. It is a cheaper strategy with limited losses compared to straddle because of the options which are purchased out of the money.

Iron butterfly strategy. Iron butterfly strategy involves selling and purchasing an at the money put and also at the money call. All of the options normally have the same expiration dates on the asset. It is named after a creature because the short put and call are offered for sale at the middle strike price forming the body part of a butterfly, while the wings come into formation when the put and call options are purchased either above or below the middle strike price. Most traders use this strategy when they believe there will be no changes in the stock's price within the time of expiry. You have a higher likelihood of getting huge profits when you are near the strike price in the middle.

Iron condor strategy. It is an options strategy that involves the sale of out of the money call and put spread on a similar instrument (preferably asset) with a similar date of expiration. It is created when the trader offers the out of the money put for sale and purchases another one of a lower strike price. Also, created by offering one out of the money call for sale and purchases another one of a higher strike price. The call and put spreads are normally of the same width. Many traders prefer this strategy because of the capability of generating huge credit on the same risk as compared to other options strategies.

Long call butterfly spread. In this type of strategy, a trader normally utilizes both bull and bear call spread strategies with three different strike prices on similar instruments and time of expiry. A trader normally purchases two contracts for options where

one is of a greater agreed price than the other contract. Also, there is a sale of two other contract options at a price in the middle.
The price agreed should be equivalent to the amount you get when you distinguish the top strike price and the lowest one.

Protective collar strategy. This strategy is exercised when you purchase a put and conversely write a call with the situation of out of the money in the market. It takes place on a similar stock with a similar time of expiry.
Combining long put and the short call forms the collar of the stock, which is normally established by the agreed prices of the options. Its protective feature, moreover, comes up from the capability of the put option to offer protection on the stock until on the expiration of the option.

Bear put spread trading strategy. A trader on this strategy buys put options at an agreed price then offers a similar amount of put for sale at a lower price. A similar type of option is on the same stock with the same date of expiration.

Most bearish traders use this strategy with the expectations that the price of the stock will drop. The advantage of this strategy is its ability to offer minimal losses though it also offers minimal profits, which is a turn off for most traders.

Bull call strategy. You, as an investor, purchase calls at an agreed price and simultaneously offer the calls for sale at a greater agreed price. Normally happens in similar instruments having a similar time of expiration. Most bullish traders use this strategy expecting there will be an average increase in the price of the stock to gain profits.

Long put trading strategy. It is a bearish options trading strategy. An investor who uses this strategy expects the stock will move become lower before the time of expiration. Risks involved here are minimal to the amount of premium paid. The downside of this strategy is that the price of the asset must drop before the date of expiration, or else you lose all the option money.

Short put trading strategy. Unlike the long put options strategy, a short put strategy is utilized mostly when the trader is bullish about the stock, that is, expects a rise in the stock's price. In any case, the agreed price becomes lower than that of the asset; then, the trader makes massive profits. The losses incurred here are unlimited.

Why Use Options?

Why should you use options? Here are a few reasons why you should utilize options as your tool for trading.

- You only need minimum initial cash outlay to purchase options as compared when buying stock in trading.

- Options such as call options enable investors to enter the market at a cheaper cost.

- Options also help investors to generate more income. It is seen mostly by using the covered call options trading strategy. The investor holds on to the stock believing the price will have few changes. As in, either to remain stable or increase a little.

- Purchasing calls and put options enable traders to invest with minimal risks since the major thing they can lose is premium.

- Using options will offer you more investment alternatives since it is a flexible trading tool.

How Options Work

After knowing the strategies and the reasons why to use options, let us now know how this type of trading works. Below are some of the details I have for you:

- Options have a time frame. They always have their date of expiration. You should be able to know their time frame to make profits. After they expire, you do not have the right to purchase or offer stock for sale at a specified price. The shorter the time it has till expiry, the lower the value of the option.

- Options have different strike prices, which normally indicate the price of the stock.

- Options offer you the right to purchase or offer stock for sale.

- Purchasing an option gives you the honor to purchase or offer the stock for sale.

- Selling an option gives you the honor of delivering the stock at an agreed price. The stock's current price is not under consideration.

Types of Options

Market options have different types and categories. Standard types include calls and put options. Other options are classified based on securities, date of expiration, the styles they are using, and many others. We shall take a look at all of the categories in this section.

- Put option. It is an option contract where a trader holding this contract has the honor of offering the instrument for sale with an agreed future price. A trader normally purchases this option with the belief that the price of the asset will fall in the future. Holders of put incur limited risks, unlike other options.

- Call option. It is a contract that enables a trader to buy an instrument at an agreed future price. A trader normally purchases this option believing there will be an increment in asset price. Call options have their benefits, which include improved efficiency in the costs and also reduced risks.

- Exchange-traded options. It's a common options contract type. Any contract is considered to be an exchange-traded option if it is on the public traded exchange list. Any trader can exercise this type of option.

- Over-the-counter option. Over the counter option is a complicated option contract. Normally happens in the over the counter market by private parties and not the general public making it less accessible.

Options based on the terms of the contracts are:

- American-style options. It isn't about the location. Options normally come with their date of expiration. American style option gives you the right to purchase or offer the asset for sale before any time of the date of expiration.

- European-style option. This type of option is different from the American style option. Here, the holder of the option contract possesses the right of purchasing or offering an asset for sale on the date of expiration and notany time before. This option is better than the American style option as it gives you some value.

Types of options based on the securities include the following:

- Stock option. A stock option is an option type mostly based on the asset called shares in a public company.

- Index option. An index option is quite

similar to the stock option. It is mostly concerned with indexes and not assets. The holder of this option can purchase or offer indexes for sale at an agreed price before the date of expiration. Indexes in the market include Wilshire 5000, Nikkei 225, and many others.

- Currency option. In this type of option, the holder of this contract has the right to purchase or offer any currency at a certain rate for sale.

- Commodity option. Commodity option is a type of option that provides holders of the contract the honor to purchase and offer futures contracts for sale at a given strike price before the date of expiration.

- Futures option. Futures option offers the owner the honor to purchase and offer a certain future contract for sale at a given price before the date of expiration.

- Basket option. It is a type of option that offers the contract holder the honor of purchasing and offering for sale a group of market securities at a given price before the date of expiration. The group of securities may include stock, commodities, and even currencies.

Below is a list of the different types of options categorized according to the date of expiration:

- Regular option. A regular option is a standard type of expiration cycle options. It gives the holder of this contract different months of the date of expiration. The months are normally four. You can select the month of expiration you want based on your preference.

- Weekly option. A weekly option is quite similar to the regular option. It, however, gives the holder of this contract a shorter time for the date of expiration. It is also limited to some market securities and indices, unlike a regular option.

- Quarterly option. This type of option is quite similar to a regular option. The difference is that quarterly options expire on the last day, unlike regular options, which expire on the last Friday of the month.

- Long-term expiration option. As the name states, a long-term expiration option normally expires in January. It takes three years before it expires, unlike the other options in this category.

Other types of options include the following:

- Employee stock option. Employee stock option is a type of option given to employees of either a public or a private company. It is given to employees as a bonus to compensate or retain them. The holders of this contract have the right to purchase some units of the capital of the company involved at an agreed price within a specific period.

- Cash-settled option. A cash-settled option is applied when it is difficult to transfer an asset to the other party in the market. There is payment in cash of the profit made by a market participant of the contract to another one.

- Exotic option. An exotic option is a customized option with complex features, unlike other options. It takes place in the over the counter market. Some of the different types under this option include:

° Barrier option. It is a type of exotic option that offers an amount to a holder of the contract when the price of the underlying instrument reaches or even surpasses the fixed one. Barrier options are less expensive and result in higher profits compared to other options. However, traders do not exercise them on the public, and due to the barrier features, they have maximum trade risks.

° Binary option. It is a type of option which provides the holder of the contract a fixed amount in any cases of profit made before the date of expiration. These options have higher returns as compared to other traders. Binary options trading platforms are user-friendly for the less experienced traders to use.

° Compound option. It is a type of exotic option that allows another option as its asset. Seen in the cases of a combination of calls and put options. Some of the benefits of compound options are that they are cheaper and have higher leverage as compared to other options.

° Lookback option. It is an exotic option that offers you the golden privilege of setting a market price by reviewing the prices of the asset and take advantage of the one with the biggest difference. A holder exercises this exotic option over the counter. The advantage of a lookback option is that it reduces risks in the market within the time given. However, this type of option is highly costly to execute in the market.

° Chooser option. It is an exotic option that enables a contract holder to select either a put or a call when the date of expiration reaches. These options have similar strike prices and the date of expiration. Chooser options are of European style.

Cons of Options Trading

- It is a complex type of trading.

- Options trading is very ambiguous. Traders need to observe the best and worst-case scenarios keenly to generate massive profits. It is time and energy consuming mostly for the less experienced traders who are not aware of the different strategies that you need to implement.

- Most traders also have no idea of the volatility of the prices in the market.

Furthermore, it is tough to get information on options trading in magazines.

- Any gains made in this trading are all taxed. The tax rates are so high for the traders ending up getting less money from the trading.

- Options have an expiry date. Buyers participating in options trading should be aware of the expiry date. The value of an asset decreases with time to its date of expiry. Many traders fail to observe this ending up purchasing assets with less value.

- Options trading has high commissions for the amount invested. The commissions for this trading can also be higher for spreads.

- Risks involved in options trading are

unlimited. You need to be alert all the time and observe market behavior.

- Options are available only to some market securities, unlike stock trading. It makes it tough for most traders.

Chapter 3:
How to Start Options Trading

There is always a beginning of everything we do in life. In this chapter, I will take you through on some of the ways on how to start options trading, some of the strategies needed for newbies of options trading, and also, the capital needed to start on this type of trading.

How Much Capital Is Needed?

After knowing how options trading works as from the previous chapter, do not rush to waste on your cash. There are too many risks in this type of trading. Capital is a basic requirement to start any business. Does options trading require too much capital? No. When starting on options trading, it is better to start with small capital to avoid massive trading risks.

Many are the individuals who utilize much of their cash for trading during their first days, which is so dangerous. Such individuals end up having too many risks to handle, and finally, they make up their minds to close their businesses. I do not want you to fall into such a mess. Do your thing with the right speed.

Start options trading with a reasonable small amount. Do not brag off that you got everything under control. You will lose even the only cash you had. Starting with less money has a high likelihood of fewer risks in trading. I bet you can now handle a few risks and be able to continue with your trading.

Strategies Used by Beginners for Options Trading

Options trading has a wide variety of strategies. There are simple to complex strategies that you can implement in options trading. Beginners find it tough to know the best simple strategies to utilize in their trading. You do not need to worry anymore. I have provided a detailed list below of the different simple options trading strategies you can use:

Buying calls. Buying calls is the simplest options trading strategy for beginners, investors, and even professionals. Investors prefer calls so much because this strategy provides them with the honor to purchase stock at a certain agreed price with a minimum amount of capital within an agreed time before its expiry.

Most of the bullish traders use this options

strategy. When there is a rise in the price of the stock, you earn good profits. This strategy is right for any beginner who wants to generate better income, earn huge profits, and even save on the trading capital.

Its great potential to massive profits, however, makes it have a bigger exposure to the trading risks. You, as a buyer, can know the risks involved in your trading. Also, buying a call strategy has a better and secure feature, which can handle many risks.

The major drawback of purchasing calls is associated with the time of expiry and the loss of value. They always have a time of expiry, so you need to check on the timing. Call options lose their value when their time of expiry reaches. You do not earn any dividends when your options are past the date of expiry.

Buying put. Buying put is another simple strategy, which is just the vice versa of buying calls. Most investors use this expecting the stock's price will fall within that time before expiry. Investors always gain good enough profits when their prediction becomes right. The things to put into consideration when buying put options include the time you are planning to be on trade and the amount of money you can afford to buy options. Purchase put options with at least one month remaining for them to expire. Do not purchase an option with a long duration before it expires. It will lose its time premium. You do not need to buy options with a duration like one year remaining for them to expire, because you will not wait to trade an option for a whole year. So, be wise when buying options. The other consideration is all about buying options that you can afford. Do not torture yourself by buying expensive put options. You will get hurt at the end. Weigh the different prices of the put options available and select the one you can afford according to the risks involved and the size of your account.

In case their prediction fails, the loss associated with this strategy is so limited. Unfortunately, you become exposed to so many risks.

Short put. Short put options strategy is all about buying a stock at a lower price than its current cost in the market. You gain profits in situations where the stock's price remains above an agreed price within that time of expiry.

Otherwise, you incur many losses.

Conversely, in situations where the stock's price falls below the price agreed before the time of expiration, another party on trade sells you the stock at the agreed price, and you have to buy it no matter the cost.

Selling a short put option is quite simple, look

for a margin account and a stock that will not drop its value any time soon. Select a date of expiration that is not that far and agree on the right price to generate more income when selling. By the time of expiry comes, you will earn good profits as long as the price does not fall.

You should be extra cautious when implementing this strategy, or else, you may lose value in your trading when things turn out unexpectedly.

Covered call. A covered call is one of the preferred options strategies for beginners. It is mostly suitable for traders who have expectations of small changes in the price of the stock or no changes at all within the expected time of expiry. A trader using this strategy normally purchases around 100 shares (unit of capital) of the stock and sells a call option against the unit of capital. After selling the option, you acquire option premiums and decrease the cost of the share. If the price of the asset behaves unexpectedly in the market, meaning that it becomes greater than an agreed price, there should be the sale of the asset by the owner using the agreed price.

Married put. A married put is an options trading strategy quite similar to the insurance policies we normally have at our homes. The strategy enables an investor who owns a stock, to purchase a put option on the stock to protect it against loss in value in the price of the stock.

You should buy the stock and put options on the same day. Also, you need to inform the options broker that the delivery of the stock you purchased will happen after the exercise of the put option. Marriage put strategy is normally used by bullish traders when buying their market trades who want to shield themselves from unlimited losses.

The drawback of this strategy is that it is costly to implement it on your trading portfolio.

Cash-secured put. On this strategy, traders write put options, and at the same time, put aside a sufficient amount of cash for buying stock. The benefits of this strategy are that you can decide on the price you want when you implement this strategy. Also, you receive payment of the options premiums when you sell cash-secured put options. In situations where the stock's price falls below an agreed price, the trader incurs too many losses.

Protective put. A protective put is an options trading strategy that many bullish traders implement to shield against loss of an asset, which is mostly caused by the drop in the price of an asset. A trader holds on to the long position of a stock and then buys a put option at an agreed price closer or equal to the price of the stock.

If it declines, the put options normally protect the agreed price (strike price) within that duration until the time of expiry. Remember, options have a date of expiration. In scenarios where the price of the stock rises, the trader involved gains good enough profits. However, the profits reduce in cases of the options cost and also commissions. Another drawback of buying puts is that the total cost of the put normally surges due to the cost of the options.

You are supposed to offer the put options for sale in scenarios where the agreed price becomes greater than the stock's price after the time of expiry. However, this leaves the asset unprotected. Alternatively, a trader can also offer the put options for sale and purchase other options.

Collar strategy. Moderate bullish traders who formulate this strategy hold shares of an asset while at the same time, purchase put options and offer call options for sale. Both the put options and call options in collar strategy have a similar time of expiry.

It is also applicable to traders who are just writing covered calls to earn premiums and also want to protect themselves from the unexpected declinein the price of a stock.

A collar strategy normally limits losses in trading but also, unfortunately, limits the gaining of huge profits. You can make more profits without this strategy in cases where the price of the stock rises.

Now, with the idea of the simple options trading strategies that exist,you should sit down, think, and select the best strategy to use as a beginner.

Weigh the risks and rewards of the strategy you will choose for excellent performance in options trading.

How to Start Options Trading

Now with the basic knowledge on options trading, I will provide you with a few details on how to start options trading journey.

1. You should look for an options trading broker. The key to successful options trading is your broker. There exist legit and non-legit brokers in options trading. Some of the tips for selecting a good broker include the following:

- *Do some research on the broker first.* You need to be keen and alert before opening a brokerage options trading platform. Different brokers will approach you with different platforms. Do not rush or assume everything is good; do some research on the best brokers. Make sure you spend your cash well by paying for a good options trading platform. It will help you a lot because your trading performance depends on your platform. Choose a broker with good ratings.

- *Charges lower commissions.* Some brokers tend to exploit traders by charging high commissions to beginners. You should weigh different commission offers of different brokers before settling on one. Some even charge no commission to traders. You should prefer brokers with fewer commissions. Payment of high commissions periodically can mess you up with losses, and you may find it even hard to secure your trading capital. Do not accept to pay high commissions. You also need to do some savings other than wasting money while paying commissions.

- *A simple user interface platform.*

There is a wide variety of software with different functionalities and features. Some software has a simple user interface, while others are too complex for you to use. You should choose a platform with a simple and clear user interface that enables you to do your trades with less struggle. Some platforms can waste your precious time when you struggle too much searching on the Internet on how you operate them.

Make your work easier by handling software that is according to your level.

- *Trading tools for research.* You should also consider factors like tools that are present on the platform. Do not purchase a platform with no tools. It will be hard for you. Platform tools ease your trading and make your performance excellent. The tools here may include charting tools, research tools, and even tools that alert you on any market changes that may arise.

- *Do some testing on the brokerage platform.* Do not be that kind of a careless trader who does things for the sake of doing with no precautions. You need to be cautious enough since this is an income-generating activity. You should test on a brokerage software before making up your mind of purchasing it. Check on the reliability and stability of the software and be 100% sure that this is the platform you will use for your trading. Ensure the software is not that type of platform that crashes down unexpectedly. You might miss crucial trade while fixing your software.

1. Be approved to trade options. You need to be approved by the broker in charge before purchasing and offering options for sale. They normally have their ways of approving you, like checking your experience and the money that you have. It

aids in avoiding risks for the customers. You cannot escape this step.

2. Get a clear understanding of the technical analysis. Options trading is a technical field. You need to have the technical analysis techniques of trading options. The technical aspects include reading charts, know about the volume of stock, and also moving averages. Trading charts mostly analyze price behavior in the market. You will handle the aspects many times while trading. Perfect your technical knowledge and be cautious with them.

3. Take advantage of mock trading accounts. Using real accounts when starting options trading is a risky game. You can lose a lot of cash within a short time duration. Mock accounts exist for a reason. You should test your trading skills in the mock accounts, learn a few tricks, and perfect your skills. The advantage of using a mock account is that

there is no loss of money since they mostly provide virtual money. It prepares you for real trading. You should take advantage of them and learn a lot. Utilize them for a while and do some evaluations on your returns. When everything works out well, face real trading and shine.

4. Utilize limit orders. It is risky to rely on market prices since price behavior change with time. You should utilize limit orders when trading. A limit order is a type of order that enables you to purchase market securities at an agreed price. Using this type of order shuns you from incurring losses in options trading.

5. Revise your strategies with time. After entering into the options trading, with time, you need to revise your strategies. Utilize the working strategies more often and get rid of unsuccessful trading

strategies. You should not have many strategies that do not bring good performance. Few working strategies are better than having multiple ones that do not help you.

6. Register and join in options trading platforms. Joining forums comprised of other options traders is another way of how to get started in options trading. Forums are platforms of different people with different experiences and opinions. You can learn mistakes made by others in trading. It is part of growing in options trading. So why shouldn't you give it a try?

7. Study and learn about trading metrics. Having your returns maximized is also another way of getting started in options trading. Traders normally use different trading metrics such as delta, gamma, theta, and vega. You should learn and practice

them for massive returns.

Chapter 4:
Tips Beginners Can Use for Options Trading

Starting something new can be tough sometimes, and it is the same case for options trading. With no tips for this type of trading, you can even give up from proceeding with it. In this chapter, I will explain some of the simple tips you need to know and also show you how options are valued.

Simple Options Trading Tips

Options trading tips are guidelines that lead you on how to do trading. Most traders make great mistakes by skipping off the options trading tips. They end up making great losses leading to the fall of their businesses. Do not be like them. Below, I have provided you with some simple tips for options trading that can assist you with greater profits and investments.

1. Be persistent and motivated. Options trading is not easy. Many despair on their way and think of doing something else. It takes time before you begin getting huge returns and cash for investment. You need to be persistent. Sometimes, things may go the wrong direction from your expectations, so never get tired. Read a lot to feel motivated in trading options and everything will be okay.

2. Hard work. Hard work pays, and it will never go unrewarded, as they say. The saying also relates to options trading. Options trading needs you to be hardworking and focused enough to excel. Trade at the right time at the right speed. Buy and sell options to get premiums. Be alert on any changes in the market. Putting enough effort into trading will help you a lot, and you will never have the feeling of giving up.

3. Never get tired of learning. Options trading is wide. You need to do a lot to prevail. Learn from other traders and be aware of the mistakes you make and that of others. Mistakes are part of the game. Learn from them. Learning is a process, and it needs determination and willingness for you to grasp something new. By doing this, it will widen your knowledge and skills in trading, and you will be brave enough to face trading.

4. Have a lot of practice. Options trading is a technical field. Technical fields require much practice for you to become familiar. It is the same for options trading. You need to practice a lot to understand all the basic concepts and tools. Making it a routine will help you a lot, and you will be able to solve any issue that may arise.

5. Manage your risks. Risks are another major issue in all types of trading. They will frequently occur when you not keen on trading. You need to always have a strategy of handling them to save your options trading capital and returns. Know how to manage your risks the right way to enable progress.

6. Utilize the options metrics in your trading. Risks in options trading can undergo modification and measurement by the use of metrics. The options metrics are normally referred to as the Greeks. Greeks help you in measuring your risks in options trading and also show you how profits and losses behave. The Greeks include Delta, rho, gamma, vega, and theta.

- Delta is not a constant metric. It normally estimates the rate at which options change when the stock's price experiences change. Delta tends to increase when you are closer to the time of expiry.

- Gamma, on the other hand, estimates any changes on the delta metric that results due to the effects of stock's price. Gamma is normally at its highest value in situations where the price of the asset is equivalent to an agreed price. Contrarily, it's at its lowest when the option has only the intrinsic value.

- Theta tells the decay duration of an option. It shows the rate at which the value of an option decreases as time goes by.

- Vega measures the value of an option and its price due to the changes in price volatility in the market.

- Lastly, the rho metric estimates the change in the price due to the change in the risk-free interest rate.

1. Take advantage of the tools and resources available. Different options trading platforms have different features. You should place the priorities for software with tools and resources integrated into them. Take full advantage of the resources. Resources such as mock accounts will help you to sharpen your skills before starting the real trading. They will assist in knowing all the necessary tricks. Tools such as charting tools and tools for analysis will assist you in reading and observing any market changes that may arise. Your trading will have good performance, and you will be up to date.

2. Options trading is simple. Everything becomes simpler when you are doing it the right way. Placing trades the right time, buying and selling the right options, reducing risks, and also implementing the best options trading strategy will make your options trading simple.

3. Shun from overtrading. Trading all the time with no breaks is unhealthy. Your mind needs time to relax and to freshen up. Make reasonable trades within a reasonable time. Do not trade a huge amount of options within a short time. You will mess up. Trade for at least one hour, take a break, and continue after around 20 minutes. Decide on which options to trade.

4. Have a strategy for an exit. Having an escape plan with you is very crucial. Sometimes you have your plans, but things

end up going south. Do not start crying or feeling defeated. You need to have a strategy of how you will bring things back to normal. Go back to your drawing board, customize your plans that are not working. Get back to the options trading game and do the right thing.

5. Move with the current situation. Normal businesses have ups and downs. You should be able to go with the flow and have a flexible mind. It is not easy but you have nothing else to do. Prices in the market fluctuate a lot. Be aware of any changes in the market and stay updated since options trading depends on the current situation in the market.

6. Begin trading with a little cash. Do not show off with your huge amounts of money when starting options trading. You might end up being a laughing stock after all. Start

options trading with little money to avoid huge risks. Do not lose your money when you are just a newbie in options trading.

7. Do great research. Researching expands your knowledge. There are a lot of newsfeeds and videos about options trading. Make use of them. Do good research in options trading for better performance. Brokers will not assist you in everything; you need to think of yourself and save yourself from failure.

8. Select a good broker. Another great tip is the selection of a good and regulated options trading broker. Options trading is done through online brokers. Most traders are not aware of this and end up being scammed by the unregulated brokers in the market. You should be very keen. Look for online brokers who are recognized by the financial authorities and check on their ratings. Some of the brokers that are recommended include

IQ brokers and expert brokers. Also, consider checking on what the broker offers in the trading platform. Go for the platforms with amazing features and educational guides for an easier time in options trading. Select a broker that charges cheaper commissions that you can afford.

9. Possess an options trading schedule. Having a schedule for yourself will discipline you in your activities. You will know the time you need to wake up and plan your trades to avoid losing your cash. You cannot just trade anytime you feel like, it is so risky. You should also be aware of the type of options you are dealing with since different options have different times of trading; a schedule will make you generate huge profits for your business.

10. Plan your budget. Knowing your options trading budget is very crucial.

Budgets help you to have discipline on how you handle your cash. Have a budget on the amount of cash to use in trading to avoid going bankrupt. Do not use cash set aside for other things like school fees and rent in trading.

You might have issues with your school finance office and your housing agency. After planning on your budget, stick to it like glue, and everything will be fine.

11. Be aware of your break-even points in trading. Every options trader needs to have a break-even point. It is a point that the price of a stock must reach for the trader to earn some profits. It also assists an options trader to know the losses that may arise and any changes in the prices.

How Is Options Valued?

The value of options is considered by the market trades and the current price of the market trade, which tends to rise and fall. Below are some of the factors that affect the value of options in a market.

The stock's price. The price of the stock is a key factor when valuing an option. It has the capability of showing how far the price is, to the agreed price. The price fluctuates a lot, an increase in the price of the stock increases the premium of the call options but decreases the put options.

The time of expiry. Options have their time of expiry. An option buyer is not lucky with time decay because as time goes with no changes in the price of the stock, an option declines its value. Time of expiry favors the options sellers instead who normally benefit when it approaches the date of expiration. The longer the time the option has to expiry, the greater the option's value. Conversely, when you are closer to the time of expiry, the values of the option lowers with time.

Option type used. There exist different types of options in trading, as you have seen in the chapters above. The standard type is mostly calls and puts options. The two types differ a lot. The call options type provides you with the right to purchase a stock at a price agreed within the time scheduled before expiry. Contrarily, put options type provide you with the right to offer stock for sale at a price before the expiration time. These two types of options have different effects when the price changes. In situations of asset price increase, the value of the options has different effects. That of call increases while that of the put decreases.

The agreed price (strike price). Most traders normally want to purchase a stock at a lower price other than higher prices. These are seen in call options. When the agreed price decreases, call options increase in their value and vice versa.

Contrarily, when selling off stock in the market, you always want to offer for sale at a higher price to gain profits. This is in the case of put options. As the agreed price increases, the value of the put options also increases. Put options are much preferred by most traders as compared to call options.

Volatility. Volatility in the market is very crucial. It is the factor that most determines the value of an option other than the price. The estimate that calculates the value is known as the future volatility. It portrays how volatile an asset is between the time it was purchased to its time of expiry.

The likelihood of higher profits increases

within the scheduled time when there are frequent changes in stock's price as compared to small changes. When the volatility of an asset is higher in the market, the call and put options also become high. They are directly related because of the increase in the potential that arises.

Amount of dividend. The amount of dividend paid does have an indirect effect on the stock's value. The stock's price is the one affected here. When there is payment of dividends, the price of the stock declines, which increases the put premiums but decreases the call premiums.

Chapter 5:
Tools and Rules for Options Trading

The Tools Used in Option Trading

In the past days, to invest in stocks, you had to call a stockbroker to help you in stock trading, and they were too expensive. With today's technology, there are tools like the stock broker's websites and trading apps to help you in stock trading. Both professional and emerging traders would like to actively monitor the market and new opportunities and to manage their accounts and their trading activities. With the right tools, trading will be effortless and effective. We will go through the tools you can use for options trading to make trading much easier and hassle-free. We will go through the apps available and describe which are the best for options trading. A trader can access these apps on your laptops, tablets, and smartphones. The apps are tailor-made to assist option traders and other investors using options trading.

Go Options: This app is free, and the app shows the fun of options trading. The app does not involve any real money, so there are no trade restrictions. These app offers cryptocurrency for trading using options, also stocks and commodities. This app is excellent for emerging traders because it provides a 30 minutes guide for new traders to learn the trading basics. Go Options is available for Android and IOS smartphone users.

IQ Option: This app is for the more experienced traders who are adventurous. This app requires real money to use it. IQ option is available for Android and IOS smartphone users. A minimum deposit of $10 is required and a $1 investment price for real money trading. The app offer VIP and pre-

VIP accounts for users who would prefer these services. The advantage of the IQ option is, you can access your money and profits at any time since no minimum amount is required for withdrawal. The downside of the app is that you will be risking your capital.

Robinhood: Robinhood has a website and a mobile app. The app is one of the best trading apps available in the market. The app's main feature is to track your stocks and the stocks you have added to your watchlist. The app is user-friendly. To start trading, tap on the stock you which to trade, enter the trade in the app, and own the stock without any trading fees. For a regular account, you will not get access to some investments, for example, mutual funds. You will have access to stocks, ETF's and the now added Bitcoin. However, you can upgrade to a premium gold account. This upgrade gives you access to margin trading, and the trading hours are also extended.

Acorns: Acorns are the best for emerging traders. The app requires you to link your bank account with the app. It tracks your spending and purchases then transfers the data to the Acorns account for investment. This process can also be manually done. When money is deposited in the account, the app will build a stock portfolio and bond investments and bond investments. The portfolio will be based on the questionnaire you filled when signing up in the app. The app focuses on ETFs to build a portfolio to go parallel with the investment goals you have set.

Stash: The best app for beginner level trading for their investment decisions. It is a trading and investment app. This is the best choice for your needs.

Stash charges $5 to start investing, it offers

assistance in what to invest and gives you more information on your investments. The app also has essential articles and tips to help you improve your investment knowledge. Your finances go into single stocks and ETF's, which are incorporated into different investment themes. Stash also has a built-in investment coach.

Stockpile: With Stockpile, you will be able to buy and sell stocks. You can also gift single shares or buy a part of the shares with a minimum of 99-cent trade fees. Using your account, you can be able to purchase high-valued stocks like Google, and Amazon using the fractional trades. And you won't have to pay $1,000 or even more per share. You will also have the option of buying a portion of stock for the lower cost of your investment. Stockpile is very suitable for families because of the buying and gifting shares of a stock feature. Kids, teenagers, and the whole family can have portfolios and can be able to teach your family the importance of investing, and this can become a family activity. Teach your children about money and investment at an early stage, and buy shares or gift them with some stocks. By engaging them, they will be able to grow a valued portfolio.

Charles Schwab: The app enables you to manage your investment and also bank accounts all in one app. Schwab also has a feature to allow you to transfer funds, deposit your checks, and manage your finances. You are also able to buy and sell stocks, ETFs, and mutual funds. Schwab is a favorite with international travelers because it offers a checking ATM card whenever the travel with no extra fees. Schwab is user-friendly; you can log in to your Android, Apple, and Kindle fire devices to check your investments. You can also pay bills on the app.

TD Ameritrade: The app is very user-friendly and straightforward to navigate. It is suitable for new option traders. TD Ameritrade offers 24/7 access to customer support via the phone and also through email support. The user can also visit their many local branches to get assistance, and the service can provide research to their users. TD Ameritrade has no hidden charges, and it does not charge platform fees, and also there is no minimum trade fee. The app charges a flat-rate commission of $6.95 equity trade and $0.75 per contract.

TradeStation Mobile: This app is one of the high rated apps, and it is free for all TradeStation clients. The users can see different options contracts with different prices and expiration dates. TradeStation app offers up-to-date information which the traders can access, and they can run options analysis, and also, the traders can view charts with various technical indicators. The app has notification features, and the traders can monitor the price changes and other indicators. TradeStation is a full-service trading app that offers access to stocks, futures options, and also forex trading.

The Rules Used in Option Trading

What are the guidelines to follow in options trading? What are the rules? These are essential questions new traders should be able to answer correctly. In this book, we will go through the rules that you should follow in options trading. And by the end of this topic, you will have the knowledge needed to trade efficiently. For a new emerging trader, these rules will be an eye-opener, while for an experienced options trader, it will be as a reminder.

These rules won't be a get-rich tip, and the

rules will help you stay out of trouble, increase your capital, and improve your money with options. Here are some of the rules used on options trading:

1. Trade small positions. When you get into the market, it's obvious to assume the worse. It only makes sense to make smaller trades and avoid big trades to reduce the risk of losing a significant amount of the money you had invested. The best tip is to make lots of small positions because if you make just one large, you risk being knocked out when you hit a loss. About 90% of options traders do not succeed because they trade large position sizes. Trading over 5% is considered a large position, and the trader risk affecting their accounts from a bad loss.

2. Don't be emotional. The market doesn't care what you think; one of the ways to be successful in trading is not to

be emotional. Don't allow your emotions to lead you, the opinions or thoughts on the market.

3. Have a high trade count. By knowing your estimated percentage chance of success, you will make a lot of trades. The higher the trade count, the higher the chances of leveling out at that expected percentage. Options trading is a number game and math, and you can pinpoint your probabilities of success in a given position. You can see your percentage chance of success; however, this can be the reason for your failure as you will have the same expectation in all your trades. So, the high trade count you make, the more consistent your percentage success rate will be.

4. Balance your portfolio. You can bet the price direction if it goes up or down when you invest in options trading. Traders tend

to focus on the investment value going up; however, you have to learn how to balance your portfolio with positions going down too.

5. Trade according to your comfort level. If you are not comfortable trading naked options or if hedged positions give you sleepless nights, then you should trade options as a speculator forming opinions and act on them accordingly. Once you are in tune with your strategies, you will realize it will be much easier for you to make money. Each strategy is unique and individual, and it might not work for all traders. By doing this, you will lower the individual's risk level.

6. Always use a model. Failure to check the fair value of the option before it's sold or bought is one of the biggest mistakes option traders make. It can be hard, especially if you don't have an exact real-time evaluation

capability. These are the basis of the strategic investment and also be aware of the bargains and the amount you are paying for the option.

7. Have enough cash reserve. It's essential to have a lot of your investment money in cash. It might be useful for brokers as they need a margin requirement when trading. They partition some amount to cover potential losses on your position. Try to keep about 50-60% of your investment portfolio in cash.

8. Reduce commissions and fees. Paying commissions and fees to transact and rebalance your portfolio might be crippling you. One of the ways to lower the percentage of the charges is by using low-cost ETF's. But for a beginner, you shouldn't pay any fees to invest in stocks.

Ten Commandments of Option Trading

One of the advantages of options trading is that you only lose what you paid for the options. However, no loss, even a smaller one, is fun. Being able to manage a loss is one of the critical keys to making money and becoming more successful in options trading. Here are ten commandments of options trading that can help you improve your options trading in the market:

1. Start with simple transactions. If you started trading in derivatives, it's unwise to get into significant option strategies. Start small with simple trades like buying and selling stock futures. Once you become more experienced with these basic future transactions, you will slowly begin buying call and put options. You have to be an informed investor to be able to start writing of call and

put options.

2. Understand the benefits. Examine future and options in a proper outlook. If you trade short in the cash market, you will have to balance off position on that day. But if it's the future, you can move forward in the short position until expiration.

3. Stops loss is a must. Most traders fail in their positions, and they never stick to the recommended stop loss. When you follow stop losses, you limit the loss if the market goes against you. Any investor who is taking a position in the Options market should abide by the recommended stop loss.

4. The brokerage myth. Low brokerage services don't always result in enormous profits. However, cheap services have low quality in the

recommendations, and it leads to weak returns after some time. Good quality is seen in the ideas with significant research. The excellent quality is expensive with a high brokerage, but it's worth it because it will bring considerable returns in the long term.

5. Don't panic when in loss. It's normal for investors to panic when they make a loss in the market. However, the options market offers enough flexibility to help you out when you are stuck in most situations. The market is tense by nature but if you have a confident advisor can help you reduce the risk of losing your investment. Here is some tips option traders can use to keep their emotions in check:

- Big picture - to be mindful of the macroeconomic and avoiding overpriced assets.
- Always have a plan for your trade - to eliminate any emotions when buying or

selling.

- Prefer bargains - look for undervalued bargains instead of overpaying.

6. Profit is what you book. Most investors get greedy in the market, mostly in F&O. It's essential that investors avoid getting too greedy and book profits when they achieve their target return. It makes sense to book profits twice than waiting too long. What you book in the market is your profit.

7. Assured return is dead. Investors should avoid looking for a guaranteed return in the Options market. It's vital to understand the options market offers benefits of the cash market with more advantages, but it's not a risk-free product.

8. Stick to one trading methodology. Each brokerage house follows and has it's own research methods, which are very different

from another brokerage. An investor needs to stick to one brokerage house to get a sustainable return.

9. Get Familiar with the terms. Without knowing the terms used in options, trading will be like flying a plane without reading the instruments. There are important insights available into the sensitivity of options costs changes in the underlying shares, making it essential in risk management. An options trader should try and familiarize themselves with the basics terms used like:

- Delta: This measures the rate of changes in parallel to the cost rate in the stock. For example, the pricing value.
- Vega: This measures the sensitive options to volatility, For example, the volatility value.
- Theta: This measures the sensitive options on a specific period, also called the option's time decay, for example, a time value.

10. Plan the trade, trade the plan. The term the disposition effect is where the investors sell their winnings too early, and they keep the losses too long; this is very common. The causes of the results are not known, but options traders can prevent this by having a plan before they start trading and executing the plan without compromising. Here are some steps you can take in planning and executing trades:

- Criteria. Have a specific standard for trading and achieving it to avoid carelessly establishing trades.
- The entry point. Set pricing you are comfortable with when paying to enter a trade and setting up automatic orders if it will need you to abide by it.
- The exit point. Before deciding to enter a trade, always have an exit point on when you would sell or determine the conditions needed for you to leave the trade open.

Chapter 6: The Best Strategies to Make Money

Good strategies of any kind of options trading are the major key to any kind of success that is about to be unfolded in any activity. Strategies are normally laid in the trading plan and should be strictly implemented in every options trading move that is likely to be involved. Let us wholly venture into the best strategies so far in options trading.

1. Collars. The collar strategy is established by holding a number of shares of the underlying stock available in the market where protective puts are bought and the call options sold. In this kind of strategy, the options trader is likely to really protect his or her capital used in the trading activities rather than the idea of acquiring more money during trading. This kind is considered conservative

and rather much more important in options trading.

2. Credit spreads. It is presumed that the biggest fear of most traders is a financial breakdown. In this side of strategy, the trader gets to sell one put and then buy another one.

3. Covered calls. Covered calls are a good kind of strategy where a particular trader sells the right for another trader to purchase his or her stock at some strike price and get to gain a good amount of cash. However, there is a specific time that this strategy should be utilized and in a case where the buyer fails to purchase some of the stock and the expiration date dawns, the contract becomes invalid right away.

4. Cash naked put. Cash naked put is a kind of strategy where the options

trader gets to write at the money or out of the money during a particular trading activity and aligning some particular amount of money aside for the purpose of purchasing stock.

5. Long call strategy. This is the most basic strategy in options trading and the one that is quite easy to comprehend. In the long call strategy for options trading, aggressive option traders who happen to be bullish are pretty much involved. This implies that bullish options traders end up buying stock during the trading activities with the hope of it rising in the near future. The reward is unlimited in the long call strategy.

6. Short call option strategy. The short call strategy is the reverse of the long call one. Bearish kind of traders is so aggressive in the falling out of stock prices during trading in this kind of strategy. They decide to sell the

call options available. This move is considered to be so risky by the experienced options traders believing that prices may drastically decide to rise once again. This significantly implies that large chunks of losses are likely to be incurred, leading to a real downfall of your trading structure and everything involved in it.

7. Long put option strategy. First things first, you should be contented that buying a put is the opposite of buying a call. So in this kind of strategy, when you become bearish, that is the moment you may purchase a put option. Put option puts the trader in a situation where he can sell his stock at a particular period of time before the expiration date is reached. This strategy exposes the trader to a mere kind of risk in the options trading market.

8. Trading time. It is depicted that options trading

for a longer period is much value as compared to a short period dating. The longer the trading day, the more skills and knowledge the trader is likely to be engaged into as he or she is likely to get the adequate experience that is needed for good trading.

Mastering good trading moves for a while gives the trader the experience and adequate skills.

9. Bull call spread strategy. In this kind of strategy, the investor gets to purchase several calls at a particular strike price and then purchases theprice at a much higher price. The calls always bear a similar expiration date and come from the same underlying stock. This type of strategy is mostly implemented by the bullish options traders.

10. Bear put strategy. This strategy involves a trader purchasing putoptions at a particular price amount and later selling off

at a lower price amount. These options bear a similar expiration date and from the same underlying stock. This strategy is mostly utilized by traders who are said to be bearish. The consequences are limited losses and limited gains.

11. Iron condor. The iron condor involves the bull call spread strategy and the bear put strategy all at the same time during a particular trading period. The expiration dates of the stock are still similar and are of the same underlying stock. Most traders get to use this strategy when the market is expected to experience low volatility rates and with the expectation of gaining a little amount of premium. Iron condor works in both up and down markets are is really believed to be economical during the up and down markets.

12. Married put strategy. On this end, the options trader purchase options at a particular

amount of money and at the same time, get to buy the same number of shares of the underlying stock. This kind of strategy is also known as the protective put. This is also a bearish kind of options trading strategy.

13. Cash covered put strategy. Here, one or more contracts are sold with a 100 shares multiplied with the strike price amount for every particular contract involved in the options trading. Most traders use this strategy to acquire an extra amount of premium on a specific stock they would wish to purchase.

14. Long or short calendar spread strategy. This is a tricky type of strategy. The market stock is said to be stagnant, not moving and waiting for the right timing until the expiration of the front-month is reached.

15. Synthetic long arbitrage strategy. Most

traders take advantage of this strategy when they are trying to take advantage of the different marketprices in different kinds of markets with just the same property.

16. Put ratio back spread strategy. This is a bearish type of options strategy where the trader gets to sell some put options and gets to purchase more options of just the same underlying stock with a similar expiration date and a lower price.

17. Call ratio back spread. In this strategy, the trader uses both the long and short options positions so as to eradicate consistent losses and target achieving large loads of benefits over a particular trading period. The essence of this strategy is to generate profits in case the stock prices tend to elevate and reduce the number of risks likely to be involved. This strategy is mostly implemented by bullish kind of options traders.

18. Long butterfly strategy. This strategy involves three parts where one put option is purchased at particular and then selling the other two options at a price lower than the buying price and purchasing one put at even lowerprice during a particular trading period.

19. Short butterfly strategy. In this strategy, three parts are still involved where a put option is sold at a much higher price and two puts are then purchased at a lower price than the purchase price and a put option is later on sold at a much lower strike price. In both cases, all put bear the same expiration date and the strike prices are normally equidistant as revealed in various options trading charts. A short butterfly strategy is the reverse wayof the long butterfly strategy.

20. Long straddle. The long straddle is also known as the buy strangle where a slight pull

and a slight call are purchased during a particular period before the expiration date reaches. The importance of this strategy is that the trader bears a large chance of acquiring good amounts of profits during his or her trading time before the expiration date is achieved.

21. Short straddle. In this kind of strategy, the trader sells both the call and put options at a similar price and bearing the same expiration date. Traders practice this strategy with the hope of acquiring good amounts of profits and experience limited various kinds of risks.

22. Owning positions that are already in a portfolio. Most traders prefer purchasing and selling various options that already hedge existing positions. This kind of strategy method is believed to incur good profits and incur losses

too in other occurrences.

23. Albatross trade strategy. This kind of strategy aims at gaining some amounts of profits when the market is stagnant during a specific options trading period or a pre-determined period of time. This kind of strategy is similar to the short gut strategy.

24. Reverse iron condor strategy. This kind of strategy focuses on benefiting some profits when the underlying stock in the current market dares to make some sharp market trade moves in either direction. Eventually, a limited amount of risks are experienced and a limited amount of profits during trading.

25. Iron butterfly spread. Buying and holding four different options in the market at three different market prices is involved in

the trading market fora particular trading period.

26. Short bull ratio strategy. Short bull ratio strategy is used to benefit from the amounts of profits gained from increasing security involved in the trading market in a similar way in which we normally get to buy calls during a particular period.

27. Bull condor spread. This is a type of strategy that is designed to return a profit if the actual price of security decides to rise to a predicted price range during a specific trading period impacting good chunks of profits made to the options trader and a limited number of risks involved.

28. Put ratio spread strategy. This strategy entails purchasing a number of put

options and adding more options with various strike prices and equal kind of underlying stock during a particular options trading period.

29. Strap straddle strategy. Strap straddle strategy uses one put and two calls bearing a similar strike price and with an equal date of expiration and also containing the same underlying stock that is normally stagnant during a particular trading period. The trader utilizes this type of strategy for the hope of getting higher amounts of profits as compared to the regular straddle strategy over a particular period of the trading period.

30. Strap strangle strategy. This strategy is bullish, where more call options are purchased as compared to the put options and a bullish inclination is then depicted in various trading charts information.

31. Put back spread strategy. This back spread strategy combines both the short puts and long puts so as to establish a position where the ratio of losses and profits entirely depends on the ratio of their two puts that are likely to be experienced in the market.

32. Short call ratio. This strategy involves purchasing a single call and later on selling two other calls at a higher price amount during a specific period of time before its expiration. This concept combines the protocols of the bull call spread strategy and the naked call strategy. The essence of this strategy is to acquire limited loss potential and mixed profits potential to the options trader involved during a particular period of time.

33. Iron albatross strategy. The particular trader gets to use this type of strategy when expecting a particular underlying stock to trade during a

particular period of time before expiration. Four transactions are usually involved in this strategy and a high level of trading is called for. This implies that this measure kind is so suitable for the experienced traders, ones who have mastered almost every market move.

34. Bull call ladder spread strategy. This one is almost similar to the bullcall strategy where security increasing in price is expected to source out some profits to the trader during options trading.

Chapter 7:
Winning Tricks for Options Trading

Financial freedom can be depicted in the number of profits that have been made in a particular period. Winning in options trading is normally reflected by the amounts of profits likely to be received at a particular time. This chapter is all about some of the ways of learning options trading and the few tips you need to know in options trading.

Below are some of the winning tricks that should be implemented while getting involved in various options trading activities.

The Tips Used in Options Trading

There are several tips that we need to abide by to achieve greatness in several options trading activities, including the following:

1. Investment tool. Different kinds of options are equated to as ways of risk- reducing kind of investment. By adhering to various options trading strategies that help in managing risks, the trader involved is obliged to invest well in options trading. Every trade measure implemented by the option trader should be measured and considered to be fruitful.

2. Options Greek. Greeks are a term in the options market that defines the different scales of risks normally involved in options trading. Some of the Greeks involved are a delta, theta, alpha, and so many others that define various risk management portfolios and other options trading activities that need to be exercised. With all these in my mind, your options trading

activities are likely to fall out in place and success be greatly pronounced.

3. Be conversant with the number of contracts involved. Several contracts are normally administered in options trading that contain different kinds of terms and conditions. Get engaged with most of the inexpensive option contracts while selling that are likely to reduce the financial costs of the entire options trading activities.

4. Capital management. Trading involves the utilization of a specific amount of capital that needs to be used in options trading. Be careful in every move you make with your cash in several options trading activities because acquiring large chunks of losses is and will always be an option in trading. Make sure options trading does not make you broke because of several misuses of funds that can be brought about by bad

management of capital.

5. Exclude expectations. Sometimes it is highly recommended that we do not try and expect any kind of results during options trading. Expected results outcomes to great disappointments. Chances of acquiring loans in options trading are known to be so low though the chances are not zero as you think they are. They are just mere, and with that in mind, you should mind on what you plan to trade with to avoid large loads of losses.

6. Selling naked options. It is much advisable to sell naked options rather than buying a stock because fewer amounts of risks are likely to be involved hence implying that the amount of monetary value to be lost is estimated to be pretty much less in various options trading activities that are likely to be involved.

7. Patience. In every trading day, there may be wins and losses. Bad days mean large loads of losses have been made, and a great financial breakdown has been experienced. You should be patient in whatever result you get to experience. Strictly stick to your game plan and follow the various strategies you have outlined. Study every move you make and learn from a great experience. Options trading calls for patience in learning and working things out. Remember that making reckless and inappropriate trading moves should not comfort you that all things are going to be okay with time, be smart.

8. Risks management. Every option strategy has a well-defined kind of risk. Before you decide on the kind of option you would like to engage in, weigh the risk tolerance of the option and check it corresponds with you. With that in mind, it becomes so much easier to handle and lay some strategies on how to

handle your kind of risks.

9. Dividends. Before initiating an option, check whether the particular option offers dividends to the stock in question during a particular period, that is before the expiration date.

10. Option objective. A set objective thrusts the trader to achieve more and motivates him or her to focus on what he or she wants to benefit from options trading. Set a big goal that should motivate you to work extra hard and achieve large chunks of profits.

11. Market volatility. This factor is famous for causing large loads of losses where stock prices just keep changing unexpectedly during trading at a particular time. Remember that losses result in a great financial breakdown.

12. Flexible thinking. The market tends to be so volatile as depicted by the fluctuations of the market prices during trading. Think of the stagnation, rises and falls of the market moves that are likely to occur during a particular options trading period. Thinking flexibly also helps you to be aware of the changes that are likely to occur in the market and the trader gets to implement various strategies.

13. Calling shots. Options trading gives the trader the chance to purchase and sell stock at their set price within a particular time. The buying, selling, exercising and other activities expose traders to various opportunities in the market during options trading. This should be a great tip and used as one of the ways of making large chunks of profits in options trading.

14. Know your break-even point. Being conversant with your break-even point

by strictly following your laid strategies that should guide you in reaching the specific price and profits be made during a specific trading period.

15. In-depth research. This talks of conducting wide and extensive research about various options trading strategies and other basic fundamental facts about it. Research allows the trader to get informed about options trading tactics, learn new skills, improve on the existing skills and master successful trading moves that would result in large amounts of profits.

16. Escape strategy. Formulating a plan and adhering to it will always bring good news. Always know when to exit the market considering the current status of the market volatility and still stick with the particular set strategies.

17. Be proactive. This one calls for dynamic nature kind of personality of an options trader where he or she is expected to check up on the trends, research, more learning. Inspect any kind of past losses and note where you messed up and get down into more ways in increasing the chances of losses made. Research, read and always strive for great progress.

18. Use implied volatility. Implied volatility is the expected volatility of the kind of stock available at the market at a particular time. Implied volatility is influenced by the rates of supply and demand currently happening at the market and as the demand increases during a particular option, the rate of implied volatility rises.

19. Self-discipline. With self-discipline, a trader is obliged to follow his or her laid strategies all the time despite the market

volatility influence. The trader can control the amount of capital involved in trading to avoid major losses that could lead to a great financial breakdown.

How to Learn About Options Trading

Remember that life stops when you stop getting educated. This part will mainly target the novice option traders that are pretty much curious and interested in how they are likely to get involved and get started with options trading. Below are some of the ways that you can consider when learning:

Udemy: Udemy is an online platform rich in educational content in various fields of several life aspects. It contains several videos and writings that may be so educational to the novice and even the experienced options traders. Go through the various learning videos and kindly take down some important notes.

YouTube: YouTube is a common social media platform and pretty much popular. Certain videos containing various levels of options trading are available, that is possible to guide the potential option trader on how to start and look into various ways in which risks are handled in options trading.

Options trading charts: Analyzing options trading charts is also one of the ways that are highly recommended by professional charts. Charts express the general statistics of the actual activities of options trading that is much to the beginners as they try to figure out several strategies that they would like to implement. Charts are also a great help to the experienced traders as they can predict what is likely to happen to the market and decide on where to put their precious money and get good guidance on what they should buy or sell.

Books: Books are pretty much detailed as compared to most of the learning sources. They provide full guidance and measures that are so much favorable to the novice traders. Below are some of the books you should consider before engaging in various trading activities:

- *Options Trading Crash Course* - This kind of book is ideal for beginners. It provides a step to step guide highlighting on the right steps a trader needs to be familiar with before starting options trading and the likely strategies he or she is most likely needed to be contented with to benefit for this new activity.

- *Options as a Strategic Investment* - McMillan's book has been rated as one of the top books overall. It entails the fundamentals of options of trading, how they normally work and various ways that you are likely to invest while implementing various strategies. This source targets both experienced options traders and beginners during various trading activities.

- *Option Trader's Hedge Funds* - This side of the book is majorly for pro options traders. This learning source gives traders the idea and motivation to make consistent large chunks of profits and huge amounts of hedge funds using various good strategies. The novice can also consider this kind of book as various ways of managing risks are also on topic.

- *Binary Options Trading* - Binary options are an options strategy that entails how traders can bet on whether the market price will rise during a particular trading period.

- *Options Trading in Your Spare Time* - This type of book is specifically written for women by experienced option traders women. This source talks of the step to step guide activities of trading activities that would be of great help to most women who have no idea how to commence or invest in a particular stock amount.

The above books are some of the common books that are used in options trading that are super important. More such books exist and are available on various sites. Keep reading.

Investopedia: This is a common financial website that is also a great learning source for the option traders. It contains various options trading fields with several constructive illustrations that have been presumed to be of great aid. Basic information about options trading to advanced is available and diverse discussions held.

ChartSchool: This is a general site for charts, where charts are analyzed, with several indicators about the current options trading activities and various chart tools. Charts equip the traders about the actual activities involved in options trading, the current trends and express the volatility of the market.

Articles: Articles have become quite common all over the Internet. Some represent detailed information about various options trading fields, while some traders get to talk of their options trading experiences and so many other things in the world of options trading.

Discussions: Online discussion has been declared as one of the ways of acquiring options trading knowledge and experience as traders get to inquire about various options trading strategies and different ways of handling various risks. Online discussions can be spotted in multiple social media like Quora, Twitter, and more. Experienced traders get to unfold their experience and teach one or two things to the novice.

Chapter 8: Money Management

What Is Money Management?

Money management is how you handle your finances, your savings, your expenditure, and investments. It is making sure you can survive a financial crisis. It means planning a budget for your long-term goals and also making investments that will help you to successfully achieve your goals. When you manage your money, you will be able to make wise purchases. Otherwise, you will always complain of having less amount of money no matter how much your income is. It can also be known as investment management.

Money management is more about risk. When you have better money management skills, you will reduce the risk. You must understand all the areas of money management to be able to avoid any risks. Plan with a negative bias, always ask yourself "what-if" scenarios, take action, and plan. When budgeting for money management, make sure you are spending less than what you save. Excellent money management will help you monitor your spending before going beyond your budget. By doing this, you will secure your savings.

You will be able to invest if you make the right decisions. Avoiding taking on more risks will help you reach your financial goals. The strategies you use in your investments play a significant role in your success. When you decide to invest, the first important thing to focus on is the risk involved, and you can avoid it. Here are some of the basics, advantages, and disadvantages of money management.

The Basics of Money Management

Money management is a wide term that involves solutions and services in the entire investment industry. You can now have a wide range of resources in today's market and also phone applications to help you manage all your finances. Investors can also seek services from a financial advisor for professional money management. Financial advisors work with private banking and even brokerage services to offer money management plans involving services like retirement and estate planning.

The Advantages of Money Management

1. Better tracking of your money. When you have a reasonable budgeting plan, you can track how you use your money, and you can monitor every expense. This is a significant

benefit to you, as you can spend less and end up saving more money. Monitor your expenses for some months and then change your budgeting by removing the less required expense and allocate that money to your savings plan, a retirement plan, or a vacation fund. Excellent money management will help you stay on track; you will be able to pay your bills on time, will be able to stay within your limit, and avoid bank account overdraws. Poor money management can put you in bad debt quicker than a blink of an eye. You can prevent those nasty fees charges when you go over your limit. By having an excellent budgeting plan, you will avoid overspending.

2. A good retirement plan. Better money management and savings plans will help you in the long term. You will be able to secure your future and have an excellent retirement plan. With better money management skills will give you a better retirement plan for you.

No matter how much you save, even when you save and invest a small amount of money, it will provide you with a more significant amount for your retirement later in life.

3. Peace of mind. Proper money management brings you peace of mind. Having bills on the counter and having no idea on how you will pay the bills or not having the money to purchase something that you needed. All these issues can be difficult to face each day. Managing your money wisely and experience all the benefits of sound money management, you will enjoy peace of mind, and you can provide for yourself and your family, too.

The Disadvantages of Money management

1. Rapid changes. With the rapid changes in the financial world, it is required to change your management plans every time. It is sometimes challenging to adjust your planning to incorporate the fast-changing situations. Unless your plan can help to adopt the new techniques, it will be limited.

2. Time-consuming. Managing your money can sometimes be a time- consuming exercise. It requires you to make the estimates as accurate as possible. However, you can use software and mobile applications to assist you with planning, and this may reduce the time you will take if you were not using the technologies. And if you have less knowledge about money management, it will take you more time to achieve this.

3. Inaccuracy. When planning, you make a lot of assumptions in terms of estimation of your expenses. Any shift like economic downturn or the change in the currency rate or interest rates can change your estimates in your planning.

What Are Money Skills?

People giving out money advice sometimes overcomplicates things. Some myths make it harder to save money and be rich, so try to forget about them. Also, some of the tips available are overwhelming and seem unnecessary.

Most successful people can balance their check without a business degree or any financial training. However, you can get by with basic information about excellent money skills.

What are these money skills that everyone should know about? Don't try to memorize all the rules. Try to understand each one of them and implement them in your day-to-day life. In this chapter, I will list down some money skills that will set you up on a path to financial freedom.

Budget without "budgeting”. Budgeting may seem like a basic thing, but it is arguably not. Only a few households keep a detailed budget. This is critical behavior, mainly if you are not hitting your primary goals–for example, fully funding your emergency fund. Luckily, you can use tools like Excel sheets and other software that are tailor-made for different personalities and requirements. Is staying disciplined in your budgeting and spending a problem for you? Consider the envelope method. From the name, this method involves having physical envelopes for your expenses and keep your cash in. This method can help you to reset your mind's bad habits. Budgeting is a process, and once your savings start to grow, you can switch to auto-deposits.

Manage debt with clear eyes. Not all debts are equal. There is student debt, which you can pay off by the increase in your income. Getting a mortgage is cheaper than renting. Some of these debts can be an investment in the future; however, you still have to make a plan for tackling these debts.

There are two methods of paying off your debts, and both ways use snow metaphors. One of the methods is the avalanche approach, where you start with the highest-interest debts first. The other one is the snowball approach, where you start with the smallest and easiest debts to pay off first. The avalanche method is usually the best to choose in terms of saving. Let's say you have $43,000 of debts of car loans, student debt, and credit card debt.

When you use the avalanche method, you will end up saving up to over

$1,000 a month sooner on interest payments. However, the snowball method is also appealing. If small victories keep you going, then you can consider choosing this method. It all depends on your personality.

Have a written plan. Financial freedom is a choice. The financial decision you make today will determine how close or far you are moving from your financial goals. Write down a financial goals plan, and this plan will guide you throughout your journey to financial success. The written plan is not about writing down some motivation words through your plans. Instead, write more detailed information defining every aspect of your financial goals and include illustrations and exact words and figures. Define your timeline and quantum of your money management to achieve your financial goals.

Start right away. Start your savings earlier to be able to achieve your financial success and start planning your retirement. You don't have to be a financial guru to begin. With early savings, you will have enough time to grow your savings rate.

Don't touch your social security. Do not tap into your social security no matter what urgent your need is as social security should be the last option. Social security is to be used after your retirement, and this means you might meet your daily expenses with your social security amount. Your pension would be better if you wait longer before you claim your social security.

Plan your risks. The higher the risk, the higher your returns will be. However, this doesn't mean you should rush into a high-risk investment with thinking twice. Based on someone's financial status, each person can afford to take risks differently. So you need to evaluate your financial situation and if you can handle a loss financially. By doing this, you will have a clear image of the risk you can afford to handle. Capital preservation should be your top priority when planning for your retirement. Access your risk profile before investing.

Plan your taxes. Between your income, expenditures, and savings, one compulsory factor is taxes. As a citizen of a country, you should be familiar with the taxation laws and how your income is taxed. Use your knowledge of tax planning and try to save more on your funds. Learning Tax planning will help you when you retire, you will be able to carefully handle your investments which are liable to be taxed.

Apply the 5% rule. This is a beneficial and practical rule. It merely means that you cut down on your expenses by 5% from your top 3 expenses in your categories yearly. To be able to apply this skill, you first have to list down your top 3 expenses in your categories, then break them down within the categories, and by doing this, you will know which areas you can save money on. For example, dining out is part of your monthly expenses, and this is essential to make it to your list. You can apply this skill by, for example, if your monthly expense on dining out is substantial and makes to the list, then find ways to reduce the costs by probably packing your lunch to take with you to the office or limit the dining out two times a month. You can quickly achieve your financial goals by breaking down into habits and creating good savings habits.

Why Is Money Management Important?

Money turns to wealth when it is well-managed. It is an instrument which is used to pursue wealth. For wealthy people, having and spending money does not bring them happiness, which gives them joy is having a steady income, and they can go on achieving their goals–and being able to leave a legacy to their loved ones. Money management focuses on your habits, and your decision making can have affected the outcome in your long-term strategies. In pursuit of wealth, there are many powerful elements such as debts, risks, and taxes that can take away all the hard work you have put in to achieve your goals. This is a life skill that everyone must learn. You don't have to be financially savvy to start managing your money. There is plenty of information available to help you better understand your finances. The following are the importance of money management:

Establishing clear goals. Have a clear approach to your decision in money management to build your wealth. Making the best decision will bring you closer to your goals. Also, set some clear and realistic goals which you want to achieve and set a time horizon for achieving them. Setting up clear goals will help you track where you are, and this will help you see your progress towards your goals. Some people give up earlier due to not being able to see their progress. You can be able to see your progress and stay encouraged if you break your goals into short term milestones. Finally, have clear and quantifiable goals to help you to make clear decisions. Abandon any choices that will not get you closer to your destination.

Controlling your cash flow. Spend less than what you earn will help you accumulate wealth. You can't be financially successful if you are not tracking and monitoring your expenditure. Drawing up a spending plan and religiously following the plan might seem trivial, but it's central to the success of the wealthiest people in the world. If you own a business, your goal will be to find ways of increasing your monthly profits, which you will use to invest in for more growth. You will learn how to prioritize your spending when you have a solid money management plan and also by making the right decisions, which will bring you closer to your goals.

Budgeting. Creating a household income budget is an essential part of personal money management. Budgeting will help you better understand your cash flow, thus giving you a clear understanding of your current financial situation.

Debt management. There is proper financial education to help you understand consumer debt and how it works. There are also financial advisers and credit counselors who provide advice on how you can review your debts, your loan terms, and how you can pay off the debt quickly and stress-free.

Managing your risks. Your risk exposure increases as you continue accumulating your wealth. You might think that wealth can make life easier, but it does not. The ignored reality is that it can make life more complicated. Getting a bigger house, expensive cars, and lavish lifestyles. These bring financial exposure and the potential to lose if all is great.

Have a risk management assessment in your money management plan with also protection strategies to help prepare you for the unexpected. Some of the unintended exposure include:

- Income loss due to illness or accident
- Death of the breadwinner in the family
- Asset exposure to liability claims

Money management will provide you with a 360-degree view of your financial status, and having financial discipline will assist you in overcoming these obstacles. With a solid money management principle, you will have better control of your financial goals.

Being tax efficient. Paying taxes is a responsibility; however, there is no obligation to paying more than necessary. Most people are not aware of how much taxes they are paying and the results of the unnecessary taxes and how it affects their wealth accumulation abilities. Money management does not focus on what you make but what you get after paying your taxes. Tax characteristics of your investment and your overall portfolio must be considered. The first thing to consider is the account location, the money allocation on different types of accounts based on respective tax treatment.

Secondly, the asset location, wherein you allocate different types of investments among the different types of accounts on the tax treatment–for example, allocating your least tax-efficient assets to a tax-deferred account such as 401(k). The taxable accounts can hold in a tax-efficient investment such as low turnover funds. This will give you more options for distribution of income in the more tax-efficient retirement, thus enabling you to accumulate more wealth faster.

The 50-20-30 Rule

For someone new in budgeting, managing your money every month can be overwhelming. You need to be organized and make difficult decisions about your expenditure. You can't rely on the experience of others because income and expenses are unique for each person. You don't need spreadsheets or for you to be a financial expert to be able to understand how much you spend.

Budgeting is not all about paying your bills on time, and it also involves the amount of your expenditure. There are budgeting tools to help you to diversify your financial profile and reach your savings goals. The 50/20/30 rule is a type of budget that can help you achieve your savings goals.

Is 50/20/30 rule the best budget?

Near 70% of Americans need improvement in their financial planning, while 60% do not have a budget. Many people see a problem but don't work for a solution. Their reasons could be that they are busy, they don't like to look at their money situation, or they don't have any idea of where to begin. The 50/20/30 Rule is one of the popular methods available. Before pinning down all your financial hopes on this rule, let us look at what this budget rule means and how it works–see if this rule is the best way to budget.

What is the 50-20-30 rule?

Primary Necessities: 50% of your income - To follow this rule, set aside 50% of your income for primary necessities in life. The percentage seems a lot, but considering everything in this category, it will begin to make more sense. 50% of the income should go living expenses and essentials. These are your rent, utilities, and transportation for work. These are the essential expenses you will have to pay, regardless of where you live, work, or what your plans are. These expenses are similar in most households, and they include housing, food, and utility bills. The 50% allows you to adjust while you maintain a substantial budget. Remember, this is the total sum of the individual cost. For example, some people live in a house paying higher rent and walk to work, while other people pay lower rent but pay expensive transportation.

Savings: 20% of your income - Then set 20% of income for your savings. These are savings, debt payments, and emergency funds. The 20% category should only be paid after you have paid your essentials and before considering the last category, which is your spending. This is your get ahead category, and the 50% is the goal for essentials while the 20% should be your goals, your obligation. If you devote more of your income in this category, you will be able to quickly pay off your debt and move towards a stress-free future. At 24 years old, when you hear the term "retirement," you might not have a sense of urgency, but, in decades to come, it will become more pressing. The earlier you start, the earlier you will earn compound interest, which will grow your funds.

Personal: 30% of your income - This is the last part, and this part makes changes in your budget. These are the needless expenses that enhance your lifestyle. It depends on your goals in life and the sacrifices you want to make. Many things fall into this category, that's why the percentage of this category is more significant than your savings. Some of these personal lifestyles include cable bills, visits to the coffee shop, and mobile phone plans. If you travel for work, then a mobile phone plan can be a necessity than a luxury. Other personal lifestyle includes gym memberships, vacations, and dining out. Designating an expense is a personal thing as you are the one who can decide which expenses are a necessity or an obligation. Similar to, 50% should go to your important expenses, and 30% should go to personal spending. By reducing these costs in your category, you will be able to pay off debt and be able to secure your future.

Establishing good budgeting habits will help you in life. You can follow the 50/20/30 rule even if you earn a low income. This is a percentage-based system, and no matter how much you make, the same proportion will apply, whether you make a lower salary, you are established in your career, or you are planning to buy your first house. Something important to note is that don't take the 50/20/30 rule too literally because each one's life is different from someone else. This plan is just a framework to guide you. Review your income and expenses, determine what is essential, and then make a solid budget plan to help you manage your money well. And in the future, you can still use the rule to guide you as your budget will continue to change when your life changes.

Money Management Problems to Avoid

Research shows an increasingly growing interest in people learning about retirement and financial planning. This is excellent news; however, most people don't save enough for their retirement. About 18% are on the right track to reaching their income retirement goals and 4% average national saving rate, which is below 10-15% the recommended saving for retirement by financial planners. It is very common to encounter some problems with money management even after getting your finances together for many years. These problems can be significant and can be simple sometimes, the everyday difficulties everyone gets at one point in their lives. However, by practicing and learning, you will be able to avoid these problems n the future.

The key is avoiding money management problem, to have peace of mind, and be able to save more money. Here are some of the problems that you should avoid to achieve a successful financial future:

1. Living from paycheck to paycheck. If you are already broke on Sunday and you were to receive your salary on Friday, then there is a huge problem. Aim at having enough money in your bank to take care of your living expenses for the next 3-6 months. Ideally, you will have enough money to cover 8-2

months to cover you during the hard times. You will be required to set aside money from each paycheck and save it in the bank. You can consider having a savings account so as you can make direct deposits. By doing this, you will avoid money problems in the future when you encounter issues like loss of a job, illness, or a home renovation.

2. Spending more than what you need. You probably dine out a little too often. Buying many lattes every week. Are you going to the movies a little too much? All these small things add a strain to your pocket in the long run. The small purchases add up to a high cost if you are charging them into your credit card. You can choose other low-cost ways of achieving this–for example, carrying your lunch and coffee and minimize dining out or buying coffee every day. All these small changes will help you in the long term. Cut down on the needless expenses to avoid this money problem.

3. Poor investment choices. Looking for ways to make huge money faster, like the get rich quick schemes, will only put you into more debt. To make money, you have to save money even while in debt. You can consult a credit counselor to help you plan to pay off your debt while you are saving through a smart budget.

4. Not having a savings plan. You should have a budget and a saving plan, no matter your age or your level of financial knowledge. Write down your finances and save the plan. Start tracking your net income. You can use mobile applications like Personal Capital and create a saving spreadsheet. By doing this, you can know where you are overspending, which area you can save more, and be able to make better financial decisions. Creating these spreadsheets will help you improve your finances.

5. Having only one source of income. One thing that can bring money problem is having only one source of income. To be able to be financially secured and successfully build a savings and retirement portfolio, you need to have more than one source of income. For example, many very wealthy people have many income streams. Don't rely on the stability of the 9-5 work only because the company might do down, and you are left with no job and a source of income. You might have some savings to cover your expenses while you look for a job, but all this can be stressful. You can consider freelance work as a source of income, and you can start a blog or rental properties. Having a side hustle will help you a lot when you lose your full- time job.

6. Misusing your tax return money. Many people misuse their tax return money on

needless expenses and forgetting to spend that money on their debts and other emergency savings. By saving this money, you will be able to increase your savings and offer some relief to your debts. It might not be exciting, but you will be setting yourself to a more secure financial position.

Money Management Strategy

This is about responsibly managing your money and having stable finances. Maximize your savings by implementing a money management strategy. The strategies range from aggressive to passive, and it depends on your initial approach. Aggressive strategies include greater leverage and broad profit goals. And passive strategies include capital preservation. Here are some of the money management strategies you should be aware of:

1. Budget and adjust accordingly. The first step in managing your finances is by creating a budget. Many people ignore budgeting because they find it hard to estimate their spending, and they have the numbers to use a starting point. It is very common for the actual numbers not be spot on, but budgeting will help you be more mindful of your spending and what you can do to improve. The more practical way is to figure out how much is your income and deduct the monthly fixed expenses. These expenses include rent, insurance, transport, and food. These expenses are constant every month, so you can easily predict them. By creating a budget, you can to compare your actual numbers and the monthly or yearly expenses. You will be able to have an accurate budget with time and experience.

2. Save for retirement. Have a great investment plan, but don't forget to plan for your retirement. Find retirement plans where you can charge your retirement. Talk to a financial advisor or a bank and find out your options. You can decide to set up a SIMPLE 401(k), SIMPLE IRA, SEP-IRA, or employer-sponsored 401(k) plan. Research of these plans and choose the one that meets your retirement goals. You don't need to deposit a lot of money towards your retirement account. By saving over some time, it will help you to control your tax bill and tax-defer until you start accessing your retirement.

3. Establish an emergency fund. Having an emergency fund for your finances is essential to cover you during an emergency, like job loss and illness. Without an emergency fund, even small expenses like repairing a fried laptop will be impossible. You might decide

to get a short-term loan to cover these expenses, but these loans carry a hefty interest rate. The short-term loan might help you to take care of the loan, but the cost will attract more cash issues in the long run. Putting it into action, the hardest part is finding the money to create an emergency fund. From your income, find ways to cut costs or find an additional source of income to be able to make more money. Put the emergency fund in a savings account or find a money market account but do not invest the money. This way, the money will be easily accessible when you require it. Start small and grow your emergency fund over some time.

4. Remembering that time is money. For a person who is starting a new business, you first start with maybe one employee to assist you in running the business. You take care of the marketing, sales, product design, and customer service. As the business grows, you

will know the task you are good at and which part you are not. For example, taxes. You might spend more than 12 hours preparing your tax return, but what's the opportunity cost for the 12 hours. You can hire someone else to help you handle your tax return filing, and you can pay them a fraction of that. Once you have a stable revenue- generating work, busy 40 hours a week. Consider outsourcing some of the work to someone else. For example, hiring an outside accountant to keep your books in order, hiring a virtual assistant to take care of your emails and marketing.

Apps Used in Money Management

To successfully manage your finances, you must first understand your cash flow. How much is being deposited in your account, and what are your expenses? These are essential parts of financial success. The good news is that there are a lot of money management apps to help you check your bank account, track your expenses, and run an analysis of your spending habits. There are also some apps to help you with financial decisions based on the data from your accounts. And the advantage is that you can check your financial situation on the go. You can access these money management apps online and also via your mobile devices, which makes it very easy to manage your finances wherever you are.

What do money management apps do?

There are two types of money management apps. The first one is an expense tracker. This type is most suitable for people who make a lot of deduction from their taxes. The business owners and other professionals. These apps will help you know how much you have spent on the stuff you require in your job, so you will have all the information need during tax season. The other type of money management is the one that helps you to track your expenses bills, utilities, and bank budgets. These apps will help you track your money to be able to minimize losses. This app is suitable for people who have multiple accounts and manage the accounts all at once and also pay most of their bills online.

If you own a business and you want to take charge of your business inflows, or you are looking to be financially secured, then there are apps available to help you dive in, save more money, and be financially secure! Here are some of money management apps you should consider:

1. Mint: Mint app can access your investment accounts, and also it offers a budgeting tool. Mint focuses more on budgeting, but it also provides an investing section, although with less focus. You are also able to keep a more detailed budget,

create multiple categories, and even categorize transactions. Mint allows you to download transactions from your bank account and credit cards. It also offers an analysis of your spending and gives insights into your spending habits, and this can help you improve. The app has a notification feature where it reminds you when your bills are due, and you can also make payments from the app.

2. Goodbudget: The purpose of the Goodbudget app is to work with your income per category of spending. The app mirrors the old system of budgeting called the envelope system. This works by allocating your income in various categories or envelope. And when the set balance in the category runs out, you stop spending. This app can be used by multi-users, thus making expenditures more transparent. Goodbudget is free and available on Android and iOS

versions.

3. Dollarbird: It is a user-friendly app that tracks expenses, and it uses a calendar to track and also helps to plan income and expenditures. Dollarbird is easy to use as it does not use currency, so the user will be able to know which currency to use. It has a clear and simple interface with large fonts and color-coded. The user can share the app and have joint finances with someone else. This app is suitable for individuals and business partners. It's free and available for Android and iOS users. Dollarbird has a premium option which costs $5 per month, or you can choose the $39 per year package, which is suitable for small business or groups that would like to collaborate on finances.

4. Expensify: This app is most suitable for a sole proprietor. This app will help you juggle between your business and personal finance.

You can use Expensify to track your expenses and the time you have spent on a project. The apps gather the information and sync it with the accounting software that you use. The beauty of Expensify is that you don't have to manually input receipt details. All you have to do is to take a snap of the receipt and upload the photo on the app, and it automatically captures the information. It is free per month if you upload a limit of five receipts, and you can also choose the package of $5 per month for unlimited scans.

Apps Used in Tracking Expenses

The first developed expenses tracking apps were in desktop programs such as Quicken and Microsoft Money in 1983. Currently, we have both web and phone-based apps, which assist you in achieving financial knowledge. These apps help you to track your budget and expenses. Money is essential in your expenses so you must monitor your cash inflow. There are some apps available that can help you track and handle your expenses; some apps have features like automatic invoice generation from receipts and direct payment to employees. Here are some of the expense tracking apps:

1. Zoho Expense: Zoho Expense allows effortless, quick approvals, and expense tracking. With this app, you can save digital copies of receipts and record live expenses. You can also add receipts to your reports and organize the expenses categorically. The app also has an in-built GPS tracker and maps, and this helps you log mileage on your trips. This feature is suitable for employees who travel. Synchronize credit cards in the app to manage transactions. You can also send the total expenses to your approving manager via e-mail and set a per-day rate for the employees. The app can be used offline to

add record information, and the changes will be automatically updated when the network is connected. Its an extension of the Zoho Expense Web.

2. Rydoo Expense: Rydoo is an all-round app with the best features like real- time analysis of expenses, and you can track your mileage. You can migrate to/from different platforms. Rydoo allows you to send expenses on the go, and you can send reports via e-mail, captured on a camera, and can also be sent via an external service such as Dropbox. The app as a feature that lets you scan receipts and add information about the project and payment method. Credit card statements can be analyzed to be able to match your expenses with your transactions. You can also set detailed compliance rules for your employees for accurate expense management. As mentioned earlier, Rydoo can seamlessly integrate with ERP packages

such as Microsoft Dynamic, SAP, and Oracle. It can easily migrate from other tracking systems like Concur and Expensify.

3. Abacus: Many employees incur expenses on different things, such as accommodation and travel. But the reimbursement process is tedious, involving mostly sending multiple invoices and waiting for approval. The app Abacus helps to speed up this process. The app simplifies reimbursement to your team, assists in reconciling corporate credit cards and implementation of the expense policy. Abacus draft expenses such as receipts, card transactions, and geolocation and makes sure that the records are accurate. One of the best features of Abacus is to automating expense policy and approve hierarchy. To avoid any violations, policy rules should be applied to expenses before submission. Then, the custom routing sends expenses to the matched approver. The expense is approved,

Abacus reimburses and direct deposits to the bank account. Expenses can also be sync into accounting software, and custom analysis reports will assist in identifying a trend, and it manages budgets more effectively.

4. QuickBooks: For the accounting software program, QuickBooks is the best choice. It helps you to create invoices, manage cash flow, and track profit. You don't have to be a professional accountant to use all these features that QuickBooks has. You can track invoices when in different currencies, synchronize bank account, monitor profits and loss in the business, review the bank transactions, and add to your accounting records. With QuickBooks, you can design invoices and receipts to have a business logo and provide your accountant with access to the account to be able to handle all the tax deductions. It supports many other apps which include inventory management

systems, as well as customer relationship management–this feature enhances the app functionality even further. The best feature of this app is the advanced billing tool. It helps to set up bills and record all the bills paid by check. You can also set up vendors and instantly pay multiple bills.

Can also synchronize payment solution such as PayPal.

Apps Used in Budgeting

For you to get back on track with your finances, you should set up a budget plan. Budgeting used to be complicated for many people, but nowadays, it has become straightforward due to the budgeting apps available. Download the right app for you to help you to pay off debt with your savings and future expenses. You can turn your Android or iPhone into a money management machine by using a budgeting app. These apps can also be like a financial advisor by identifying ways to save more money and to avoid wasteful spending. These apps automate functions that used to be done manually, making budgeting a simple process. They can also offer learning materials to help people with more knowledge of money management. The app contains different features and benefits, so it is essential to choose the app, which will best suit your needs. You might use a budgeting app, and over time, you outgrow it and find a more detailed one. This is common, and it means you are growing your knowledge and skills on how to manage your money. With the various apps in the market, you need to research and evaluate the app you are thinking of using.

Here are some of the best budgeting apps available:

1. Mvelopes: This is a digital envelope budget

that gives you better control of your cash. The app has been used for a long time as compared to other apps. The developers have improved the app into a great tool with unique features for all of the budgeting needs. Mvelopes has three product levels: Mvelopes Basic, Plus, and Complete. The user can put their money in different envelopes according to their financial situations. By doing this, you can account for every penny in your

budget. In all the levels, you can use as many envelopes as possible. Your digital envelope can be as detailed as you want.

Mvelopes offer live support in all the levels via phone or chat. There are resources such as personal finance trainer for consultation. Also, on their website, you can find a learning center. The app offers a variety of services as each customer has a unique requirement. Mvelopes uses Android and iOS version.

2. Unsplurge: This is an app that helps you

save up for a specific item. It's a fun app, but this can't be used as a budget management tool. You can use this app if you are planning to buy something soon, such as a car, a house, or a vacation. Unsplurge aims to help you achieve your goals, and also it monitors your progress and offers tips to assist you in getting to your goals. It works by enabling you to save money from your daily expenditure towards your goals of purchasing the item you want. This app also helps you to avoid any debt which you might have taken to buy the item. Unsplurge is free to use on the iPhone.

3. You Need a Budget (YNAB): This app is popular with young professionals. YNAB is hip and different from the regular traditional apps. It has a different approach to money management, and it focuses on four simple rules as opposed to the methods of categorization. It accounts for every cash by

giving your income a job, such as paying bills, savings, and investing. YNAB keeps it simple, and this helps to avoid the stress of setting up a full- blown budget. It plans for unexpected expenses and assists you to move ahead and avoid living from paycheck to paycheck. It prepares you to be ready when you encounter unforeseen issues. YNAB has free introduction online classes to help you improve your money management skills. The app also offers a goal-tracking feature that allows you to achieve your savings goals and your plans to pay off your debt. It works on both Android and iPhone.

4. PocketGuard: This app focuses on spending management. PocketGuard links to your financial accounts. It is user-friendly and best for budgeting and monthly tracking your savings and bills. It looks for ways you can save your money by analyzing your statements. The app also looks for current

better deals for your monthly expenses, such as phone bills and internet services. PocketGuard accounts for your future expenditures and the expected income by managing your cash flow. The app has a user-friendly interface and offers charts and graphs to clearly show your financial status. It can be used on Android, Desktop, and iPhone devices, and also on your Apple Watch.

5. Wally: Wally is not a very easy app to use as compared to other budgeting apps. However, it works well in budgeting. Wally helps you to track your earnings, your spending and provides you with a snapshot with the balance of your budget and, this helps you not to overspend. This app is more popular with young professionals. Wally is a free app to use and has an Android and iPhone version. The Android version is referred to as Wally+. The best feature is that

the app supports nearly all foreign currencies, which is an advantage for those people who live outside the United States.

You would have made a wise decision regardless of whichever budget app you decide to choose because the key to financial success is to have a solid financial plan. The best decisions in your everyday spending have the best budgeting where you will save every dollar. Track your money to avoid having debt and also to be able to pay off your debt. Having a budgeting app will help you have some savings and even emergency funds, which you can depend on when you are having problems such as illness. There is no reason not to use all these available resources to help you to manage your money.

How to Control Your Money

Not everyone can stick to a strict budget plan, and they end up been frustrated and spending even more money. It is advisable to cut back a little bit at a time so that you won't feel restricted. Here are some steps you can take to control your money:

Step #1: Get informed. To make the best decisions, you should first know your money. Understand the basics of money, what you earn, your spending, and what you can save. Be aware of your habits to be able to reach your goals.

Step #2: Set goals. Set goals to achieve more. Setting goals gives you clarity, and it doesn't matter if you are starting in your career, how much you earn, or if you are successful in your career. Having a goal will help you stop wasteful spending and save more. And it will also help you handle your debt and be stress-free.

Step #3: Get organized. Organize all aspects of your life, your money, home, office, and your kids. Involves your family and learn to stay organized when you encounter the unexpected in your daily routine.

Step #4: Ask for help. If you are in doubt or not sure about your money matters, seek advice from a financial professional. Prepare a list of questions to ask and make an appointment with an expert. You will make better decisions if you have detailed information.

Step #5: Create a spending plan. Build a plan to manage your spending.

Sticking to a plan is challenging for many people. This is why creating a budget that will match your spending patterns is essential, and this will help you avoid impulse spending. You will be able to set your financial goals and achieve them. It will give you motivation, and this is the key to your financial success.

When you take control of your money, you invest in yourself. You have to start doing things differently. There is no better time to begin than right now! Follow the five steps: identify your spending habits, set a goal, be organized, ask for help, and build a budget that is perfect for you. These will give you a fresh start and start your financial success .

Chapter 9: Tactics for Successful Trading

One successful fundamental thing and another successful thing will lead to a successful outcome. Let us venture into some of the ways that we need to get exposed to and consider so that our options trading activities can be successful.

Which Trading Is Profitable?

There are several basic kinds of options trading activities that the novice and even the experienced traders should be familiar with and get to master their favorite kinds of options trading that it is much going to be profitable during various occurrences. Here are some of the profitable ways.

1. Buy to open. This involves initiating a new order to secure a new option and eventually getting to improve on the existing trading position as judged from the past trading activities.

2. Sell to open. Selling to open is selling a specific option that you do not necessarily own and in the end, acquiring a new position or an improved position in the options trading activities.

3. Buying to close. This is buying a specific option that you had previously sold in the market and eventually reducing a position in the options trading market.

4. Selling to close. In this kind of trading, an order to sell a specific option is exercised, where whatever you are selling had been previously been bought and end up reducing or exiting an existing position in the trading market.

How to Be a Successful Options Trader

Below are some of the ways we can shine on this options trading field.

1. Risk management. Life is a risk itself, implying that risks will always be depicted. An options trader needs to master all the possible ways in which he or she can minimize the number of risks that are likely to occur and learn from everyone of it for future good management. For instance, in the capital sector, the trader ought to have a big plan entailing details on how capital should be used strictly. Losses are also part of the options trading aftermath ,and with bad capital handle, everything can tumble down. Think of how bad the market volatility can stand, leading to a great amount of capital, and leading to large chunks of losses.

2. Be the chief in numbers. Options trading involves wide use of numbers. Do you know the implied volatility? Is money in the option or out of the option? For beginners who have no single trace of what is going on, kindly commit oneself to some in-depth research and try to get a spotlight. For the intermediate and experts, keep learning about various numbers in options trading. Life stops once you stop learning.

3. Possess great discipline. Self-discipline is encouraged as you get involved in options trading. This is the up-thrust motive force that will drive you towards as per your agenda plans with so much determination. You get to follow your specific laid plans and strategies, learn so much from your trading activities, and get the respective skills and experience for more successful options trading. Remember that your set plan

strategies are the core objects during options trading, implying that self-discipline will bring you nothing but great success.

4. Great patience. Every aspect of life is a process led by constant growth. Trade during several market movements and get to learn from it. During this options trading journey, you will be exposed to various occurrences that you need to learn and master each one of them. Learn the possible risks involved, several market tricks and so much on. Well, get the best experience for it is always the best tutor.

5. Have your trading style. The intended trading style is what's normally implemented in the trading plan. Your trading style should be strictly adhered to and updated with new skills and information as you get involved in various options trading activities. Follow your plan without any other kind of influence and

watch yourself grow with options trading.

6. A trading plan. Failing to plan is planning to fail. This implies that failing will only be reflected once planning does not happen. Successful options traders have big plans. Big plans entail good laid strategies, functions, discussions, in-depth research, great self-discipline, targets, and good goals. Establishing good trading plans is a clear reflection of great success in options trading.

7. Emotionally stable. Emotions can be quite a distraction as we get involved in different aspects of our lives. Losing a trade should be viewed just like a bad day that comes in handy with a good learning experience and knowledge for a bright future. Winning days should also be a learning day by valuing the good moves expressed that day.

8. Intensive learning and being proactive. Life always remains stagnant when you stop learning. Learning is achieved from the good side and the bad side, in that, master and learn every possible move expressed in options trading and be quite interested in picking the essence morals from the past episodes and squeezing any goodness from it. Also, subscribe to various well- contented channels and blogs to get the wide knowledge that is needed in options trading. Learning makes you informed and educated on the actual trade activities that are commonly involved in options trading.

9. Secure, accurate trading records. Try to learn from your mistakes though it can be tricky at times to formulate straight decisions based on your past performance since options trading is a matter of happy and sad seasons governed by several set strategies that have been correctly laid in the options

trading plan. It is encouraged to learn from your past mistakes and get to grow strategically to become a successful options trader.

10. Determination and commitment. This entails the high thrust force that should govern a beginner or any kind of experienced trader to acquire what is best for him or her in options trading and getting to know the several tips on becoming a successful options trader.

11. Be flexible. Another point to add is that when you feel that the market does not suit you at all that particular options trading period, find something constructive to do. Master any possible market move that is likely to take place in options trading and master it.

12. Basic understanding and interpretation. The trader should familiarize himself or herself with the basic market terminologies to understand the basic activities of the market and get to know the various ways on how to begin and handle option trading. Interpretation involves getting to analyze the actual options trading happenings in the market and sourcing the essentials in every trading activity. This helps the trader to always look out for the reality of the market rather than the hype and depending on the major market deadlines.

13. Be aggressive. Being aggressive in options trading essentially implies that there is a thirst for great success, and the chances of acquiring large amounts of profits are so high. An aggressive option trader is mostly partaking in- depth research learning new and learning new lucrative trading moves. This gives the trader much experience and skills to face any

kind of risks that are likely to be involved in the market and, within no time, the trader has accredited a great expert in options trading.

14. Emotionally stable. The trader involved in options trading should not be controlled by various feelings experienced in the market. The losing days should not discourage the trader in any way such that he or she decides to stick with the market hype. It is highly recommended that traders should follow their plan and always stick to their various strategies.

15. Good stock pick. An options trader needs to pick the right option to sell. Weigh whether you are capable of handling the respective stock and managing the necessary risks highly involved in it. Most importantly, is the stock going to benefit the trader from acquiring large amounts of profits?

16. Good capital management. Money is really important when it comes to trading. Monitor and plan for every amount of capital you plan to utilize in the market. Always be careful in the amount of money you place in every option. Acquiring losses is always an alternative when it comes to option trading, a breakdown that can tumble you so badly and make you bankrupt as well. Plan for the capital you plan to invest in the company.

17. Powerful trading platforms. The kind of platform where various trading activities are taking place is pretty much important in any kind of options trading involvement. Your best platform should consist of awesome navigation tools, learning sources, and other amazing features.

18. Selling options. Selling options is mostly preferred rather than buying

options while practicing the call and put strategies that eventually help the trader to gain a good amount of profits.

19. Correct timing. As a trader, you should be informed of the good times and the bad times. Enter the market when the timing is quite favorable. Bad timing leads to great amounts of losses being made at the options trading market leading to a great downfall of finances. Bad timing leads to great amounts of losses being made at the options trading market leading to a great downfall of finances that, after all, causes bankruptcy.

Strategies to Be Successful in Options Trading

Good strategies set in the options trading plan should be prioritized. Back testing, measuring and weighing the current laid strategies by comparing them with some former historical records and learning the growth and the happenings that have happened in the recent periods, is highly recommended by the expert traders. Major strategies are going to be discussed later on in the book but meanwhile, let us peep at some of the strategies that should be considered:

Use a proper time period. A longer period, for instance, five years, is recommended during in-depth research and during analyzing the various sources to lay some good strategies. Remember to pick a quite long period to get the actual information and report in all that as part of learning.

Covered call. This kind of strategy involves both trading on the underlying stock and also to those of the options contract. The end goal of a covered call is to collect income through the premiums and majorly selling the stock amount that you already possess. Below are some the ways you need to consider in creating a covered call:

- Purchase a stock and buy it in the form of shares.
- For every 100 shares you own, sell a call contract.
- Then hold on for the call to be exercised.

The kind of risk involved in covered calls holds the stock position carefully that could fail with time. The large chunks of profits of this particular call are equal to the price of a specific call option and a lower purchase price of the underlying stock.

Market put. This strategy involves the trader had made two purchases of stock trading and that of a put option. The benefit of this is that you, as an options trader, can shield oneself from several losses occurrences. The market put is also considered advantageous during purchasing a security that is bearing a bullish outlook. The market put strategy is also essential when protecting depreciation in particular stock prices.

The market put is also referred to as a synthetic long call due to the similarities in the number of profit potentials on both sides.

Options spread. This strategy is established by selling several options and purchasing options of the same class and from the same security with various strike prices and expiration dates.

Butterfly spread. Butterfly involves four calls and puts and also considered as a market-neutral strategy that gets to pay most of its underlying stock without the concern of the expiration dates involved.

There are several varieties of butterfly spreads that normally use four kinds of options with three different strike prices. To add, different kinds of butterfly have different levels of the maximum profit amount and the maximum loss amount that are normally experienced during options trading.

Short bull ratio strategy. Short bull ratio strategy is used to benefit from the amounts of profits gained from increasing security involved in the trading market in a similar way in which we normally get to buy calls during a particular period.

Bull condor spread. This is a type of strategy that is designed to return a profit if the actual price of security decides to rise to a predicted price range during a specific trading period impacting good chunks of profits made to the options trader and a limited number of risks involved.

Put ratio spread strategy. This strategy entails buying several put options and purchasing more put options with different strike prices and of the same underlying stock during a particular period.

Strap straddle strategy. Strap straddle strategy uses one put and two calls bearing similar strike price and with an equal date of expiration and an underlying stock that is normally stagnant during the particular trading period. The trader utilizes this type of strategy for the hope of getting higher amounts of profits as compared to the regular straddle strategy over a particular period of the trading period.

Long straddle. This is also known as buy straddle, which majorly involves buying put and call options of the similar underlying stock and bearing the same striking price and equal deadlines that have been involved during options trading. Long straddle options normally involve unlimited profits with reduced risk management options that are implemented when an option trader in question feels worse concerning the market volatility rates.

Long strangle. Commonly referred to as buy strangle, this is purchasing slight options derived from similar underlying stock and bearing equal due dates in the same period. Long strangle options also experiences large chunks of profits and benefits and fewer risks are likely to be involved during the actual trading.

Bear put spread strategy. This kind of strategy involves purchasing a put in the belief of gaining from an expected downfall that is expected to be impacted in the underlying stock and extracting another put in the same expiration and a much lower strike price to cover for some of the costs that have been experienced.

Protective collar strategy. This kind of options strategy protects the trader against so very big losses but, at the same time, it ends up limiting the trader from gaining large loads of profits and benefits. An investor initiates a collar by purchasing a put option and the same every minute he or she is initiating a call option.

Bull call spread. This is a kind of an options trading strategy fit to gain from a stock's increase in its actual price. Two call options are normally involved and a defined range is established between the highest strike price and the lowest one.

Cash secured naked puts. This kind of strategy involves writing at the money or out of the money and setting a particular amount of cash aside to purchase stock.

Iron condor strategy. This strategy involves the bull call spread strategy and the bear put strategy all being utilized at the same time during a particular trading period. The expiration dates of the stock are still similar and are of the same underlying stock. Most traders get to use this strategy when the market is expected to experience low volatility rates and with the expectation of gaining a little amount of premium. Iron condor works in both up and down markets are is believed to be economical during the up and down markets.

Married put strategy. On this side, the options trader purchases where the strike price is and at the same time, gets to buy another share of a particular stock. This kind is also known as the protective put. This strategy is also a bearish kind of options trading strategy.

Cash covered put strategy. Here, one or more contracts are sold with a 100 shares multiplied with the strike price amount for every particular contract involved in the options trading. Most traders use this strategy to acquire an extra amount of premium on a specific stock they would wish to purchase.

Long or short calendar spread strategy. This is a tricky kind of strategy present in the options trading market. The market stock is said to be stagnant, not moving and waiting for the right timing until the expiration of the front-month is reached.

Collar strategy. A collar strategy is established by holding several shares of the underlying stock available in the market where protective puts are bought and the call options sold. In this kind of strategy, the options trader is likely to protect his or her finances used in the trading activities rather than the idea of acquiring more money during trading. This kind is considered conservative and rather much more important in options trading.

Bear put strategy. This strategy involves a trader getting to purchase multiple put options at a specific strike price and later on end up at a much-reduced price. These options have a similar expiration date and derived from the same underlying stock. This strategy is so common to the bearish kind of traders who benefit from the limited losses and gains experienced during that period.

Albatross strategy. This kind of strategy aims at gaining some amounts of profits when the market is stagnant during a specific options trading period or a predetermined time. This kind of strategy is similar to the short gut strategy that is still implemented in the options trading market.

Chapter 10: Mistakes to Avoid in Options Trading

Trading is not an easy thing. Most of you do not know that. You just start the business with no plans, tips, and strategies. How do you even expect to survive? Entering into the options trading game with so much excitement, forgetting the crucial things you need to do will lead you nowhere. Mistakes eventually arise, and you become stranded on what to do. In this final chapter, you will be informed of some of the mistakes traders commit and the ways you can shun from those mistakes.

Common Options Trading Mistakes

There are several common mistakes that traders commit while trading options. Below is a detailed list you can go through it.

1. Lacking a trading plan. Most traders enter into the options trading game without a plan. You have got a high potential for loss. Failure to organize yourself into trading is preparing to fail. Without guidelines, you cannot make it in trading. All your goals of making money will be destroyed. When you buy or sell that option, you will be incurring a lot of losses.

2. Lacking an exit strategy. When your plans fail to work out, what do you do? Do you just implement rushing decisions on your trading? An escape plan comes in handy here. Having an exit plan is very crucial in all trading. You can control your profits and losses. Most traders fail to have a detailed escape plan, which makes them fail tremendously. You lose all your money and fail in trading.

3. Having ignorance at the time of expiry. Options have a date of expiration. It is an important factor when purchasing calls and buying put options. Most traders fail to recognize this factor and end up messing up the last minute. Options lose their value when you are closer to the time of expiration.

4. Buying options with the mentality that they are cheap. Cheap is expensive. Cheap options have lower premiums compared to the expensive ones. You will earn little or no cash with cheap options with many losses. Options that are out of the money are not friendly at all, especially for beginners in options trading.

5. Selecting the wrong trade. Working on a trade that you cannot handle can land you into big trouble. There is a high potential for bigger risks. Work on the trade you can

manage to succeed. Putting effort into complex stuff than your ability is a total failure. Many traders who get themselves on the wrong trade lose a lot of their money and precious time.

6. Depending on guesswork. Too much guesswork in options trading is a risky game. Guesswork like the rise and fall in the stock's price is not an advisable strategy. You should take advantage of the tools of research, analysis, and education materials. Tools for analysis help in analyzing outcomes in a detailed manner as compared to guesswork. Education materials will empower your knowledge a lot in trading, and you will be aware of the basic concepts. The research tool will assist in the formulation of strategies to be used in trading. The use of guesswork will surprise you a lot with the trading failures.

7. Ignoring protective stop loss. Failing to have a stop loss is a really bad idea. You can fail tremendously in trading. Most traders who prefer to cheap options, wait to go out of the market when the option becomes fruitful, or it declines when it reaches the time of expiration.

8. Being over-optimistic. Optimism is always acceptable though being over-optimistic is another bad idea. Options trading is all about performing some mathematical calculations and coming up with the right figures for your returns and losses. Putting a positive mind always is not healthy in trading since many risks are involved here. You need to be prepared for the losses that might occur and be ready enough to handle them.

9. Using only one strategy. In the chapters above, there exists some information about

the many strategies you can implement in options trading. You need to go through the many strategies before deciding you will settle on which strategy. You not advised to rely on only one strategy. Having different strategies will help a lot. In case one trading strategy fails yet you are in a critical situation, you can implement another successful strategy as quickly as possible. Your trading will experience no delay. You should consider mostly the simple and crucial strategies that are needed to be implemented in all options trading. An example of the strategies is the covered call strategy.

10. Trading with a bigger bite. What's all with the rush? A successfulmoney- making procedure requires smaller and sure moves other than big and weak moves. Take your time in trading and go at the right speed. Do not be so greedy for the money that you make complex decisions ending up losing

everything. Good things take time. You need to accept that fact. When you utilize much of your cash, there are higher chances of bigger losses other than just spending a little money.

11. Lacking persistence and consistency. Trading is not like any other business that makes a huge amount of money just in the few days after entering the business. First and foremost, trading is tough and risky. You need to persist with all the risks and also be consistent. Most traders give up when there are occurrences of risks in trading. Keep pushing hard and of course, everything will work out fine.

12. Failing to accept uncertainties. All markets have imperfections. Failure to accept the things you cannot control in options trading is a big loss. Market uncertainties will always be there, be ready to accept them and look for something else that you can control

to save your time and money. Worrying a lot into something not useful is not advised in options trading.

13. Lacking trading goals. "By the time the year ends, I want to have…" These are the kinds of goals all options traders need to have. Who out there works out for things with no goals? Goals are the things we wish to have or do. Failure to have clear and realistic goals in options trading is a turn off to being successful in options trading. You need to have goals that you are working for. Traders who lack goals do not have the motivation to achieve something greater. Most of them do things for the sake of doing it. They trade at any time and use their money recklessly. Lacking goals leads to the failure of the options trading.

How to Avoid Common Mistakes

Mistakes are always in the game. You need to find yourself some strategies and ways to survive in options trading. Mistakes are part of the learning process. You should learn from your mistakes for growth and improvement the next time you are trading.

Do not be emotional when you commit mistakes in options trading. You will get carried away by the emotions and end up doing things of no importance. Go through your mistakes and see where you went wrong. Put much effort next time and avoid the mistakes to succeed.

Below is a detailed list of some of the ways on how to shun from common mistakes in options trading:

1. Possess an options trading plan. Test the plan after formulating it. If it works, it is well and good. Stick to it. It helps in organizing your trading patterns. You will be able to estimate your profits and losses. A tradingplan makes you disciplined and responsible for trading. You will know your moves during your worst-case scenarios while trading options. Implement your working strategies according to the plan.

2. Work with a different and reasonable number of strategies. Do not relyon one strategy. It is dangerous. Arm yourself with several successful and crucial options trading strategies to be on the safer side when market imperfections decide to play along. Strategies assist you on how to do your things in trading and provide protective measures.

3. Take good advantage of technical tools provided to you by your broker. They enhance a quick understanding of options trading and understanding the basic concepts. They also ease the trading process since most of the trading platforms are online software.

4. Do not spend much money when placing trades, especially when you are a beginner. Begin from a small amount since the risks involved here are minimal. Do not utilize all your cash when you are a newbie only to end up losing everything. Take care of your money since you worked hard for it.

5. While trading, utilize the disposable income that can easily be refunded. Do not reach for your school fees or money for food. The risks involved in options trading are huge; it is tough to refund the money you lost. Using the money for food to placing

trades will lead to starving and lack of school fees. Be wise when dealing with this trading.

6. You need to have realistic and achievable goals that you want to accomplish when starting off options trading. Goals are there to motivate you in trading. You will always put effort into trading to succeed what you desire.

7. Enter into a trade that you can manage. Many individuals will mislead you on the internet on the types of trades. Stick to your plans and select the types of trades good for you. Getting yourself into many and complex trades will stress you a lot.

8. There are different types of options such as binary options and many others. You should decide on the type of option you will settle with. Do not be the trader who deals with everything. Things will go out of control and you will lose everything.

Decide on the option you more interested in and perfect that skill on the market.

9. Traders should be serious with the factor of time of expiration. The time of expiry is related to the value of an option. You should be alert and select options with a longer duration to expiry for your option to have a high value. You will be able to gain profits and massive returns.

10. Consider volatility in the market. It will save you from a lot of trouble in the market. The metric, implied volatility, can tell how volatile the market will be in the future. The metric can tell the amount of options premium you are capable of generating. You should, therefore, make use of the implied volatility in options trading.

11. Practice a lot in options trading. Have a routine of when to place your trades on the

platforms. Study more on the best time to perform your type of trades in the options trading market. Practice will make you get used to trading with time which is a tip for successful options trading.

12. Have an escape plan for yourself. Do not start trading without an exit plan. This strategy saves you from losses when the market is experiencing worst-case scenarios. It guides you on the actions to implement at dark times which are better than the closure of a business.

13. Buying not-cheaper options are preferred to sticking to only cheaper options. Cheaper options have no progress in trading; they have lower options premiums as compared to the expensive ones. You should buy good options to earn more. Check on the quality of the options before

purchasing.

14. Tend using protective measures in options trading. Measures such as covered call strategy assisting in protecting your trading capital and prevents you from risks in trading.

15. Have flexible options trading strategies. The change in stock price is normally unpredictable. Its behavior may not align with your strategies. You should have the capability of altering your strategies to align with the current market situations. Test on the new strategy that you encounter, if it works out well, implement it on your trading for massive returns. If it does not work out well, the best thing to do is to drop it and find a better solution.

Conclusion

We believe after going through all the chapters, sub-chapters have been engaging, and that you have learned a lot. At this point, your confidence level has improved and you are ready to start trading. Even if you are a beginner or an expert, this book can always be your point of reference in case you are stuck. Some tips and illustrations have been used to make sure that you clearly understand and apply all that.

Start by looking for the minimum capital and set up all the minimum requirements; do not be scared to start small and grow as you gain more experience. Follow all the laid down rules and ensure you have the effective tools to be successful. When you start earning, you must know how to manage your money as well as its basics and importance, and the apps that can help in budgeting, money management, and tracking your expenses. The tactics can also help you to be successful in options trading, and keep in mind the common mistakes to avoid.

www.ingramcontent.com/pod-product-compliance
Lightning Source LLC
LaVergne TN
LVHW011521200926
848484LV00001B/103